The Olympic Tour
of China

Seeing Sports, Venues, Cities
and Parks All Together
in Beijing, Shanghai, Tianjin, Qingdao,
Qinhuangdao and Shenyang

TABLE OF CONTENT

TITILE: The Olympic Tour of China: Seeing Sports, Venues, Cities and Parks All Together in Beijing, Shanghai, Tianjin, Qingdao, Qinhuangdao and Shenyang

ISBN 978-0-9761183-3-6

Special quantity discount or sample copies for promotional sales may be available from Agilceed Books. For more information, please write to the Sales Manager, Educational Publishing, Agilceed Books at 8181 Oakley Lane, Avon, IN 46123. For information on bulk purchase prices, translations or book distributors outside the U.S.A., please contact Agilceed Books at agilceed@gmail.com.

Photo Credit: The Beijing Organizing Committee for the Games of the XXIX Olympiad

June, 2008

PREFACE

WELCOME TO CHINA AND ENJOY OLYMPICS

China is a large country with over 5,000 years of history. China's economy has grown rapidly after China opened the door to the outside world. Today, China is one of the most important economy entities in the world.

Now, for the first time ever, China is going to host the 29th Olympics Games. This world famous sport event will attract many foreign visitors to China. We are going to tell you that you won't regret coming to see the great Olympic Games you like in China. Why not carry your country's flags and support your country's athletes? Why not use your own eyes to see the real China?

Even when the Olympic Games are over in China, you can still visit these fantastic Olympic venues. China has spent a lot of money on these great architectures such as National Stadium (Bird's Nest) and National Aquatics Center (Water Cube).

During your travel in China, you will have the opportunity to see many travel attractions in the Olympic co-host cites including Beijing, Shanghai, Tianjin, Qingdao, Qinhuangdao and Tianjin in mainland China. You will also witness the rapid progress China made after the economic reform. The modern China may be very different from what many people heard or thought in their own country.

In this book, we show you how to travel in these Olympic host cities and give you a lot of useful information to make your trip as smooth as possible. The book is organized as follows.

Chapter 1 gives you some information about what you need to before your travel in China.

Chapter 2 talks about the 2008 Summer Olympics including tickets, sports and schedule.

Chapter 3 introduces to you the transportation, money, telecommunication, etc.

Chapter 4 describes different Olympics sport events in 29th Olympic Games.

Chapter 5 gives you some guidance about where to go to see the travel attractions in the Olympic host cities.

Chapter 6 introduces different types of Chinese food and entertainment you can enjoy.

Chapter 7 talks about shopping in these Olympic cities.

Chapter 8 mentions some practical travel tips.

Hope this Olympic tour guide book is useful for you and best wishes to your travel in China!

1 PLANNING AN OLYMPIC TRIP

Getting Visa

Are you thrilled about seeing the Olympic Games in China? Will you be visiting these great places at the conclusion of the Olympic Games? You will need to acquire a valid visa before you enter the People's Republic of China.

You can apply for tourist visa to travel in China as long as your country has normal diplomatic relationship with People's Republic of China. The tourist visa type is "L" type. A traveler can apply for the tourist visa in Chinese embassies and consulates in his own country. Usually you only need to wait for less than 5 working business days to get a standard 30-day single entry visa. In some cases, you might get the visa within one day. It will be valid for entry within 3 months. If you do not have time, you may ask your travel agency to apply it for you. If you joined a group tour of more than 9 people, then the organizer can apply for group tourist visas.

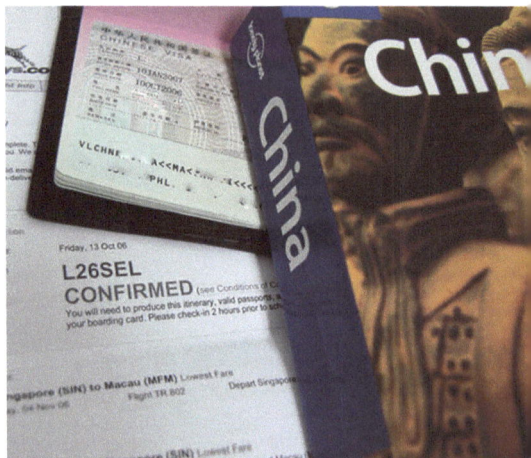

※ It's important to note that you can't visit China if your passport is expiring within six months of the day that you enter the country.

Any person who intends to visit China longer than one month period is required to apply for visa extension from the local authority. The local Public Security Bureau (Gong'anju) handles the processing of visa extensions. It might be possible for your visit to be extended by 15 to 30 days. The fine of at least 300 Yuan per day will be issued to travelers overstaying in China, after their visa expiration. If you want to visit Hong Kong from mainland China, then you need a double or multiple-entry visa to gain re-entry to the mainland China. Please note that the visa policies may subject to change at times and you need to get latest information from the Chinese embassies in your country.

Foreign visitors should always have their valid passport and tourist visas with them as they travel through China. You'll need to prove your identity when you arrive at your hotel, purchase transportation tickets, or exchange currency. Foreign visitors to China, who have tourist visas, need to abide by Chinese laws, and avoid forbidden activities like getting a job, demonstrations or handing out religious propaganda. The government in China will protect the legal rights of visitors to its land.

※ *China is not currently fully open to foreigners. If you want to go to those areas that are not open to the outside, you have to obtain permits from Public Security Bureau.*

If you lose your passport while in China,
you must go to the nearest Public Security Bureau immediately. You can also ask the embassy or consulate of your country for help in China. In Beijing, one Public Security Bureau in Beijing is located in 85 Beichizi Jie, near the famous Forbidden City. Do not overstay after your visa expires. There will be heavy penalties associated with it. You are required to register your place of residence with the local Public Security Bureau within 24 hours of your arrival. If you will stay in a hotel, normally this registration is done for you by the hotel when you check in.

Booking Hotels and Airline Tickets

There is a large variety of hotels, from five-star to "court-yard" hotels and youth hostels. You can find well-known western hotel chains if you prefer their international standards of service. These prices can be quite costly, and they'll probably go up during the Olympic Games in 2008. Chinese-run hotels are usually less expensive and the quality of their customer service has improved a lot. Additionally, you can obtain major discounts of up to 50 percent at a Chinese-run hotel. Choosing a Chinese-run hotel might be your best choice if you're on a budget. For an easier experience, make your hotel reservations ahead of time.

You may request that your travel agent make arrangements for hotels. If you'd rather book your own hotel, then you can begin your search online. You can go to the websites of western hotel chains that have properties in China and make your reservations online or by phone. There are two Chinese online travel search engines that can offer discounts to travelers looking to save some money. **CTRIP** and **ELONG** are the ones you want. Both of these firms provide lists of hotels throughout China, and have English web pages so that tourists can search through their listings. You'll be surprised to know that their prices are cheaper than what you'll discover on Expedia or even on Kayak. You're able to book your hotel online, and when you do, you can pay by major credit cards such as MasterCard or Visa. Each hotel has in depth information on the site, including facts about availability and price. Using this strategy will get you a much cheaper hotel price than physically visiting that hotel. CTRIP has a website just for the 2008 Olympics related tour promotions and hotels. (http://pages.ctrip.com/commerce/promote/200805/aoyun/portal2.html)

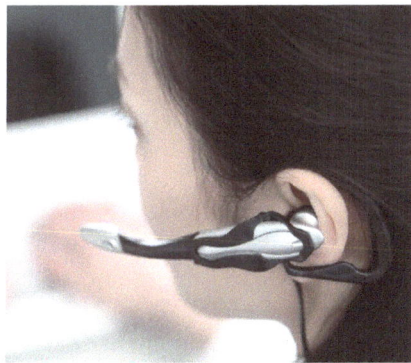

CTRIP also offers international flight deals. Call ☎ 400-8206666 from mobile or call ☎ 800-8206666 from a fixed phone line to talk to an English-speaking operator.

The following are the contact information for these two companies. Both of them have offices in Beijing and Shanghai. You can use any of them to arrange your hotel and airline tickets during your travel in China.

CTRIP

Shanghai (Headquarter):

No. 99 Fu Quan Road,

Shanghai, PRC, 200335

Tel: (8621) 34064880

Fax: (8621) 54261600

Beijing:

6F-G Office Tower A, East Gate Plaza No. 9 Dongzhong St,

Dongcheng District

Beijing, PRC, 100027

Tel: (8610) 64181616

Fax: (8610) 64185833

Website: http://english.ctrip.com/

ELONG

Reservation Hotline:
☎ 400-8101119 (in Mainland China). If you are calling from other countries, you may dial:
☎ 0086-10-64329999 extension 6.

ELONG Beijing Office

Address: Block B, Xingke Plaza, 10 Jiuxianqiao Middle Road, Chaoyang District

Tel: (010) 58602288

Fax: (010) 64315872

Email: web@elong.net

It has an airport counter located opposite to No. 8 Gate of Terminal 2 at the Beijing Capital International Airport. ☎ Tel: (010) 64590451 / 13801069232

ELONG Shanghai Office

Address: 1/F, No.10 Multimedia Valley, Lane 777, Guangzhong West Road, Shanghai

Tel: (021) 61071010

Fax: (021) 61071300

It also has an airport counter located in No.305&306 counter,Arrival Hall of Terminal A, Hongqiao Airport.
☎ Tel: (021) 51152046

Here we give you a few hotels to choose from in different Olympic cities. Remember you can find a lot more choices on the ctrip or elong websites.

Beijing

Comfort Inn & Suites

Address: 4 Gongren Tiyuchang Dong Lu

Tel: (010) 85235158

Scitech Hotel

Address: 22 Jianguo Men Dajie

Tel: (010) 65123388

Grand Hyatt Beijing

Address: 1 Dong ChangAn Jie

Tel: (010) 85180000

Jinglun Hotel

Address: 3 Jianguo Men Wai Dajie

Tel: (010) 65002266

Shangri-La Beijing

Address: 29 Zizhuyuan Lu

Tel: (010) 68412211

Shanghai

The Bund Hotel

Address: 525 Guangdong Lu

Tel: (021) 63522000

Hengshan Hotel

Address: 534 Hengshan Lu

Tel: (021) 64377050

Holiday Inn Vista

Address: 700 Changshou Lu

Tel: (021) 62768888

Pacific Hotel

Address: 108 Nanjing Xi Lu

Tel: (021) 63276226

Jinjiang Hotel

Address: 59 Maoming Nan Lu

Tel: (021) 62582582

Qingdao

Haitian hotel

Address: 48 Hong Kong Xi Lu

Tel: (0532)83872006

http://www.hai-tian-hotel.com/

Huiquan Dynasty Hotel

Address: 9 Nan Hai Lu

Tel: (0532)82999888

http://www.hqdynastyhotel.com/

Dongfang Hotel

Address: 4 Da Xue Lu

Tel: (0532)82865888

http://www.hotel-dongfang.com/

Huanghai Hotel

Address: 75 Yan'an Yi Lu

Tel: (0532) 82870215

http://www.huanghaihotel.com/

Shenyang

Liaoning Hotel

Address: 97 Zhongshan Lu, Heping District

Tel: (024)23839166

Donghai Hotel

Address: 47 Changjiang Bei Jie

Tel: (024)86116341

Kailai Hotel

Address: 32 Yingbin Jie, Shenhe District

Tel: (024)22528855

Hongxiang Hotel

Address: 53 Wanliutang Lu, Shenhe District

Tel: (024)24820818

Tianjin

Tianjin Hotel

Address: Youyi Lu, Binshui Dao

Tel: (022)28359000

Kaiyue Hotel

Address: 219 Jiefang Bei Lu

Tel: (022)23318888

Web: http://www.hyatt.com

Youyi Hotel

Address: 94 Nanjing Lu

Tel: (022)23310372

Xilaideng Hotel

Address: Zijinsan Lu

Tel: (022)23343388

Lishunde Hotel

Address: 33 Tai'erzhuang Lu

Tel: (022)23311688

Qinhuangdao

Huaoqian Hotel

Address: 132 Yingbin Lu

Tel: (0335)3604466

Great Wall Hotel

Address: Yansan Da Jie Zhong Duan

Tel: (0335)3061666

International Hotel

Address: 346 Wenhua Bei Lu

Tel: (0335)3083083

Xinyi Hotel

Address: Yingbin Lu

Tel: (0335)3062243

Finding Travel Agencies

It is possible to book your airline tickets and your hotel with the help of a travel agency. In fact, they can even provide you with all the details. For assistance, you can utilize the travel agencies in your own country. Chinese travel agencies can arrange a tour of many local attractions and make your trip easier and more enjoyable once you arrive in China. We'll provide some large travel agencies in different Olympic cities for you to reference. The Chinese travel industry acknowledges each of these well known travel agencies as being reputable companies that offer quality assistance. These travel agencies are recognized for their quality of service by Chinese travel industry.

Beijing

China International Travel Service Head Office

Address: 103 Fuxingmennei Dajie St.
Tel: (010) 66011122

China Travel Service Head Office

Address: 2 Beisanhuan Donglu
Tel: (010) 64622288

China International Travel Servies (CITS)
Address: 28 Jianguomenwai Dajie
Tel: (010) 65222991
Fax: (010) 65221733
Email: support-en@cits.com.cn
Website: http://www.cits.net

China Youth Travel Proprietary Ltd.

Address: 23 Bing Dongjiaominxiang Lane
Tel: (010) 65243388

China Kanghui Travel Service Ltd.

Address: 5 Nanzhanguan Nanlu Rd.
Tel: (010) 65940856

Shanghai

ShangHai CITIC International Travel Co.LTD

Address: 1168 Nanjing Xi Lu
Tel: (021) 52925277

Shanghai Oriental Pearl international travel service

Address: 1 Pudong Shiji Da Dao
Tel: (021) 68879765

Shanghai China Travel International Ltd.

Address: 519 Aomen Lu, Huasheng Dasha
Tel: (021) 62981111

China Youth Travel Services

Address: 2 Hengsan Lu
Tel: (021) 64330000

China International Travel Servies (CITS)

Address: 1277 Beijing Xi Lu
Tel: (021) 62898899

Qingdao

China Travel Service Head Office Qingdao Co., Ltd
Address: 12 Donghai Xi Lu
Tel: (0532) 83886060

Qingdao china international travel service co.,ltd

Address: 73 Hong Kong Xi Lu, Yuyuan Da Sha, Area A, floor 6
Tel: (0532) 83893001

Qingdao Huaqing International Travel Service Co.,Ltd

Address: 129 Yan'an San Lu, Jinyi Da Sha floor 8
Tel: (0532) 83872700

Qingdao Zhongyuan International Travel Service Co., Ltd

Address: 38 Xuzhou Lu
Tel: (0532) 86685655

Qinhuangdao

Qinhuangdao ETZD International Travel Service

Address:197 Hebei Dajie, Jinyang Dasha Room 407
Tel: (0335) 3604666

Qinhuangdao Great Wall International Travel Service

Address: 132 Hebei Dajie Zhongduan
Tel: (0335) 3509002

Qinhuangdao Haiyan International Travel Service

Address: Hebei Dajie, Qinxin Huayuan A4
Tel: (0335) 3032076

Qinhuangdao Beidaihe Jinshan International Travel Service
Address: 4 Jinsanzui Lu, Beidaihe
Tel: (0335) 4033598

Tianjin

Tianjin China International Travel Service

Address: 22 Youyi Lu
Tel: (022) 28109988

Tianjin China Youth Travel Service

Address: Rongye Dajie, Xinwenhua Huayuan, Xindianju building 2
Tel: (022) 87308688

CITIC Travel (Tianijin) Co.,Ltd

Address: 18 Zhenzhou Dao, Gang'ao Dasha 1001-64
Tel: (022) 23161078

Shenyang

China Travel Service of Shenyang

Address: 189 Shifu Da Lu, building 1

Tel: 13909888832

Shenyang Overseas International Travel Service

Address: 39 Heping Nan Dajie, Jiahuang Dasha 3F
Tel: (024)31875555

CYTS Tianjin International Travel Service

Address: 166 Xinhua Lu, Haizhou Dasha 407A
Tel: (010) 58156268

Shenyang International Youth Travel Agency Co., Ltd

Address: 6 Wenhua Lu
Tel: (024) 22895505

Packing Luggage

Before you embark on your trip, here are some suggestions for what to bring along.

Having travel guidebooks may prove useful to you. You're also going to be walking a lot on your trip. Therefore, having a quality walking-style shoe is a must. If you're taking prescription drugs, bring them along, and make sure you're carrying enough to last the duration of your whole trip. Remember to bring your prescriptions with you to avoid any problems when you pass the customs. Bring your medical records with you.

Even though August isn't the hottest month, you should take heed of the strong ultraviolet radiation. In August, you can expect high temperatures to average 84 degrees Fahrenheit. Needless to say, it is wise to bring sunglasses, sun block, and light clothes to remain happy in the hot summer weather.

You should be sure to bring medicine for an upset stomach or diarrhea, since some of the food or water could make you ill. By not drinking the tap water, unless it has been boiled first, you will reduce your likelihood of this occurring. However, it is always better to be safe than sorry.

Most of the products you are used to buying at your local stores are also available in China. Nevertheless, it's also a good idea to take lots of deodorant and tampons along, because it's hard to find these things while you're traveling.

The number of bags you will be allowed to bring on the flight will depend on which airline you are flying with and which class you are traveling in. Typically, you will be allowed between 45 and 90 pounds. Some airlines may offer larger allowances for business and first-class travel passengers. By purchasing a first-class ticket you will be allowed two carry-on bags, whereas an economy-class or a business-class ticket will only permit you to carry-on one bag.

In order to make your luggage as light as possible, limit the number of outfits you bring, and use the hotel laundries regularly. You might want to consider buying much of the clothing you'll wear when to arrive in China. This is good because you'll find low prices on a large selection of quality clothing.

In addition, we suggest you get comprehensive travel and medical insurance before your travel. Check any exclusions of your insurance and make sure the policy you have can cover you for the activities you want to undertake during your travel in China.

Lodging for Less

It's imperative to choose lodging that suits you. Where should you live during the hot season? You have several options to choose from. Staying at an international standard star-class hotel is one option. If you choose a star-class hotel, it will be quite costly, particularly while the Olympics are going on. If you can afford it, you might want to consider this option in order to enjoy its many services and amenities. When the Olympics are going on in Beijing, many hotels will be at capacity. In fact, some hotels are already full well in advance. If you're looking for affordability and comfort when choosing a place to stay, we have some excellent recommendations.

First of all, try to contact CTRIP and ELONG companies mentioned previously, they can find some hotels which have rooms available and suit your budget.

Purchasing a package tour is an option. Companies like Cartan Tours (1-800-818-1998, website: http://www.cartan.com) can give you different packages, depending on your budget and hosting needs (completely guided or semi-independent). Packages generally include your airfare, transfers, breakfasts, public transportation and often other services; these run for as short as five day durations.

You can also opt out of visiting Beijing and choose instead to travel to a Olympic co-host city that isn't attracting as many visitors, such as Hong Kong, Shenyang, Qinhuangdao, Tianjin, Qingdao, or Shanghai.

An Olympics family is another good idea, if you want to know more about the Chinese culture and know how the real Chinese people live. This is probably the least expensive choice. The city government of Beijing has launched a campaign to select local families who are willing to rent their homes to foreign tourists who have come to watch the Olympics. The Olympics Families are selected according to some criteria. They have to be clean and large enough to accommodate the foreigner. The city government has arranged for prices to be between 400 and 600 Chinese RMB (about $57-85) per day, based on the number of rooms you get and whether or not food is included. The official contract will state the final price. You can find such Olympic families near to the Olympic venues. The famous travel agency, "China Travel Service Head Office" (http://www.ctsho.com/) is the main organizer of the Olympics Family program. The travel agency can get the tourist to make the most out of China's exquisite cuisine, beautiful scenic locals, and take home more than just the family's favorite Olympics Mascots. You can visit the website (http://www.ctsho.com) for further information about Olympic Family program. As the travel times will be a problem, try to consider the distance from the Olympics game venue when you book a room.

There are some cheaper motels for you to choose from. One website offers motels in several cities including Beijing. Its website in English is: http://www.ziyougangwan.com/en/index.php

Many owners of apartments, located close to Olympic sites, are also advertising cheaper accommodations. Their apartments can be rented for a brief while, between a few days and a few months. The apartments are generally clean and well-maintained and have access to some TV, Internet, etc. For further information and contact numbers, look up their website. We recommend that you visit these websites that are offered in English:

http://apartment08.com/index.htm

http://www.2008beijingfocus.com/main.asp

Another place to look for apartment for rent is craigslist. Its website is: http://beijing.craigslist.org.

2 OLYMPIC VENUES AND SCHEDULE

The First Olympic Games in China

The Olympiad which is held every four years has a history of over one hundred years and is the ultimate international sports competition. Back in 1894, with the intention of improving international relations in mind, Baron de Coubertin and Pierre Fredi decided on a sports event; so the Summer Olympics was born. In the first year only 14 countries participated with 245 competitors of which more than 200 were from Greece.

Without doubt the 2008 Beijing Summer Olympics is the biggest sporting event of 2008. Numerous events will be held in the competition with the first, second and the third competitors awarded gold, silver and bronze medals respectively.

Beijing's National Stadium will see the opening ceremony of the 2008 Beijing Olympics on August 8, 2008. The event will run to August 24, 2008. Approximately 10,500 top athletes from 100 countries competing in 302 disciplines will participate. There are other co-host cites including Shanghai, Tianjin, Qingdao, Qinhuangdao, Shenyang and Hong Kong. For instance, Qingdao city will host marathon swimming, beach volleyball and sailing while the Hong Kong sports Institute will organize the equestrian events in Fo Tan, Sha Tin.

Event Tickets

In early August 2006, the Beijing Olympic organizing committee started to publicize the sale of over 7 million tickets to the general public through various sporting events and ceremonies. Domestic tickets went on sale on April 14, 2007 through the Beijing organizing committee; they account for 75% of total ticket sales. At the same time, international ticket sales were handled by each country's respective National Olympic Committee (NOC). Approximately 2.2 million tickets had been sold by June 2007.

There are a few ways to buy tickets. Firstly, when you arrive in Beijing, there will be ticket offices outside the Olympic stadiums. It's also worth trying Bank of China to see if any of their branches have any remaining tickets for sale, but this is not a sure way to obtain your ticket. Secondly, Beijing's travel agencies will sell you tickets along with trips to local tourist attractions. Thirdly, you can buy your tickets online. Lastly, official ticket agents appointed by your respective countries National Olympic Committees (NOC), will be happy to sell you tickets. You can contact your country's NOC for details.

The following are some websites which are selling 2008 Olympic event tickets:

http://www.cosport.com

http://www.euroteam2008.com/index.php

http://www.wstickets.com/olympics/games/olympics_tickets.html

http://www.cheappremiumtickets.com

Olympic Venues

Many Olympic venues are brand new, such as the National Stadium and the National aquatic Center, these and other venues will host many exciting events during the 2008 Beijing Olympics. Even after the Olympic Games, many of these places will become tourist attractions and are well worth a visit. Below, you can find information about each venue and how to get there using the Beijing public transportation system. Without doubt, a taxi is the most convenient and direct method to get to your destination. For those on a budget or wanting to save a penny or two, the bus or subway is a good alternative. Listed below, are the nearest subway stations for most venues and how to get there by subway or bus. For your reference we also list the 2008 Olympic Games schedule.

Olympic Venues in Beijing

- National Stadium
- National Aquatics Center
- National Indoor Stadium
- Beijing Shooting Range Hall
- Beijing Olympic Basketball Gymnasium
- Laoshan Velodrome
- Shunyi Olympic Rowing-Canoeing Park
- China Agricultural University Gymnasium
- Peking University Gymnasium
- Beijing Science and Technology University Gymnasium
- Beijing University of Technology Gymnasium
- Beijing Olympic Green Tennis Court

- Olympic Sports Center Stadium
- Olympic Sports Center Gymnasium
- Beijing Workers' Stadium
- Beijing Workers' Gymnasium
- Capital Indoor Stadium
- Fengtai Sports Center Softball Field
- Yingdong Natatorium of National Olympic Sports Center
- Laoshan Mountain Bike Course
- Beijing Shooting Range CTF
- Beijing Institute of Technology Gymnasium
- Beijing University of Aeronautics & Astronautics Gymnasium
- Fencing Hall of National Convention Center
- Beijing Olympic Green Hockey Stadium

- Beijing Olympic Green Archery Field

- Beijing Wukesong Sports Center Baseball Field

- Chaoyang Park Beach Volleyball Ground

- Laoshan Bicycle Moto Cross (BMX) Venue

- Triathlon Venue

- Road Cycling Course

National Stadium (国家体育馆)

Designed by the Swiss architects Herzog & DeMeuron and China Architecture Design Institute, the National Stadium, on the Olympic Green, has 80,000 permanent and 1000 temporary seats. Nicknamed "the Bird's Nest", its area covers approximately 258,000 square meters and will become a major tourist attraction after the Games are over. As the showpiece venue of the Olympic Games, the Beijing National Stadium will host the opening and closing ceremonies of this massive world event. With a 91,000 capacity, the stadium will host the track and field events and some of the high-profile football matches.

Address: Beichen Lu, Chaoyang District.

Closest Subway Station: Olympic Park Station

Transportation

Subway: Take subway No. 10 line, transfer at Xiongmao-huandao subway staion, then take the Olympic spur line (奥运支线).

Bus: Take any of the following bus such as 113，386，407，656，737，740，753，804，827，939，944，983; get off at bus stop Beichen-qiaoxi.

National Aquatics Center (国家游泳中心水立方)

The 17,000 seat National Aquatics Center is highly regarded for its innovative architecture and its visual appeal. It will be the venue for the swimming, synchronized swimming, and water polo events. Affectionately known as 'Water Cube', the aquatic center is constructed of a steel space frame, clad with ETFE pillows. The square, which has traditionally formed the basic shape of houses in China and in Chinese mythology, has been taken as inspiration for the structure. Crystals, cells and foam bubbles inspired the design, shape and appearance of the structure. This wonderful structure will attract numerous visitors from around the world well after the 2008 Olympic Games are over.

Address: Beichen Lu, Chaoyang District.

Closest Subway Station: Olympic Park Station

Transportation

Subway: Take subway No. 10 line, transfer at Xiongmao-huandao subway station, then take the Olympic spur line (奥运支线).

Bus: Take any of the following bus such as 113，386，407，656，737，740，753，804，827，939，944，983; get off at bus stop Beichen-qiaoxi.

National Indoor Stadium (国家体育馆)

The National Indoor Stadium, on Olympics, is one of the important

venues for the 29th Olympic Games. Handball, trampoline and artistic gymnastics will take place here.

Address: Beichen Lu, Chaoyang District

Closest Subway Station: Olympic Park Station

Transportation

Subway: Take subway No. 10 line, transfer at Xiongmao-huandao subway staion, then take the Olympic spur line (奥运支线).

Bus: Take any of the following bus such as 113，386，407，656，737，740，753，804，827，939，944，983; get off at bus stop Beichen-qiaoxi.

Beijing Shooting Range Hall (北京射击馆)

The Beijing Shooting Range Hall will host eleven shooting events, including the 10 meter, 25 meter and 50 meter qualifying rounds and finals for the 29th Summer Olympics. All of the shooting sport events for the 2008 Summer Paralympics will also be held at the Beijing Shooting Range Hall.

Address: 3 Futianshi Jia, Shijingshan District

Closest Subway Station: Senlin Gongyuan Station

Transportation

Subway: Take subway No. 10 line, transfer at Xiongmao

Huandao station, take the Olympic spur line (奥运支线), and then get off at Senlin Gongyuan station.

Bus: Take any of the following bus such as 109，305，315，333，344，355，392，407，419，478，490，604，618，670，719，748，752，753，810，819，839，909; get off at bus stop Qinghe Nanzhen.

Beijing Olympic Basketball Gymnasium Center （北京奥林匹克篮球馆）

Basketball events of 2008 Summer Olympics will take place at the 18000 seat, 168,000 square meter Beijing Olympic Basketball Gymnasium Center. The preliminary and finals for both the men's and women's events will be held here.

Address: Wukesong Culture and Sports Center. 69 Fuxing Lu.

Closest Subway Station: Wukesong Station

Transportation

Subway: Take subway No. 1 line, get off at Wukesong station.

Bus: Take any of the following bus such as 115，337，370，373，436，620，624，654，711，728，740，748，751，804，817，840，913，952，967，982，983，996; get off at bus stop Wukesong.

Laoshan Velodrome (北京老山自行车馆)

Located in the Laoshan District of Western Beijing, is the 250 meter, international standard, Laoshan Velodrome. The oval arena can accommodate around 3500 excited spectators in its galleries to view the Olympic track cycling events.

Address: 15 Laoshan Xi Lu, Shijingshan District

Closest Subway Station: Babaoshan Station

Transportation

Subway: Take subway No. 1 line, get off at Babaoshan station.

Bus: Take any of the following bus such as 325，327，337，354，385，389，472，621，622，663，728，941，958，959; get off at bus stop Jingyuanlukou.

Shunyi Olympic Rowing and Canoeing Park (奥林匹克水上公园)

The 2008 Beijing Summer Olympic Games' rowing, canoeing, and kayaking events, will take place at the Shunyi Olympic Rowing and Canoeing Park in Mapo Village, Shunyi District, Beijing. It can hold 25,000 people and we recommend going there by taxi as it is the most convenient method of transportation.

Address: Chaobahe, Mapo Village, Shunyi District

China Agricultural University Gymnasium (中国农业大学体育馆)

Wrestling events at the 2008 Olympics will be held at the China Agricultural University campus, gymnasium. It has a seating capacity of 6000.

Address: 2 Yuanmingyuan Xi Lu

Closest Subway Station: Wudaokou Station

Transportation

Subway: Take subway No. 13 line, get off at Wudaokou station.

Bus: Take any of the following bus such as 110，419，628，913，963; get off at bus stop Jingshuyuan or Nongye Daxue Dongqu.

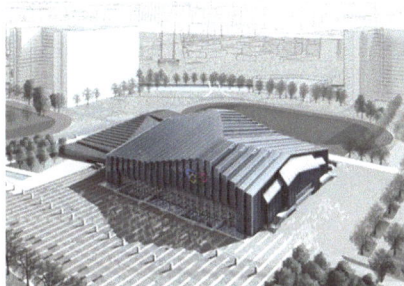

Olympic Venues

Peking University Gymnasium (北京大学体育馆)

Peking University Gymnasium is located on the southeastern part of Peking University which is located in Haidian District, north-west Beijing. This indoor arena will host the men's and women's, singles and doubles table tennis events. Peking University Gymnasium will have a floor area of 26,900 square meters with 6000 permanent seats and 2000 removable seats. When the 2008 Beijing Olympic Games are over, this venue will host national and international competitions for badminton, volleyball, handball and basketball, as well as being a center for training, physical education and recreation.

Address: 5 Haidian Lu

Closest Subway Station: Huangzhuang Station

Transportation

Subway: Take subway No. 10 line, get off at Huangzhuang station.

Bus: Take any of the following bus such as 205，307，320，355，365，498，681，716，717，731，737，801，811，826，982; get off at bus stop Zhongguanyuan.

Beijing Science and Technology University Gymnasium (北京科技大学体育馆)

The taekwon do and judo events of the 2008 Olympics will take place in the Beijing Science and Technology University Gymnasium. This up-to-date, modern indoor venue can facilitate and seat approximately 8000 spectators.

Address: 30 Xueyuan Lu, Haidian District

Closest Subway Station: Wudaokou Station

Transportation

Subway: Take subway No. 13 line, get off at Wudaokou station.

Bus: Take any of the following bus such as 307，484，630，726，836; get off at bus stop Beijing Keji Daxue Beimen.

Beijing University of Technology Gymnasium (北京工业大学体育馆)

With a surface area of 22,269 square meters and a seating capacity of 7500, the Beijing University of Technology Gymnasium's indoor venue will host Olympic Badminton and rhythmic gymnastics events.

Address: 100 Pingleyuan

Closest Subway Station: Jinsong Station

Transportation

Subway: Take subway No. 10 line,

get off at Jinsong station.

Bus: Take any of the following bus

such as 30，34，486，649，752，801，852，938专，973，985，988; get off at bus stop Beijing Gongye Daxue.

Beijing Olympic Green Tennis Court (北京奥林匹克公园网球场)

The 2008 Beijing Olympic men's and women's tennis events will be held at the Beijing Olympic Green Tennis Court. It has a 17,400 capacity with 10 courts and six practice courts. This venue will also stage the Paralympics Wheelchair events.

Address: Olympic Park

Closest Subway Station: Senlin Gongyuan Station

Transportation

Subway: Take subway No. 10 line, transfer at Xiongmao Huandao station, take the Olympic spur line (奥运支线) and then get off at Senlin Gongyuan station.

Bus: Take any of the following bus such as 109，305，315，333，344，355，392，407，419，478，490，604，618，670，719，748，752，753，810，819，839，909；

get off at bus stop Qinghe Nanzhen.

Olympic Sports Center Stadium （奥体中心体育场）

Beijing's Olympic Sports Center Stadium, a 40,000 seat, 37,000 square meter venue, will have many uses during the 2008 Olympics. The snow jumping and cross-country disciplines of the modern pentathlon take place here as do some of the football matches.

Address: Anding Lu 1, Chaoyang District

Closest Subway Station: Olympic Sport Center Station

Transportation

Subway: Take subway No. 10 line, transfer at Xiongmao Huandao station, take the Olympic spur line (奥运支线) and then get off at Olympic Sport Center station.

Bus: Take any of the following bus such as 113，386，407，656，737，740，753，804，827，939，944，983; get off at bus stop Yayuncun.

Olympic Sports Center Gymnasium （奥体中心体育馆）

Next to the Olympic Sports Center Stadium, is the 7,000 spectator, 47,410 square meter Olympic Sports Center Gymnasium. This 2008 Beijing Olympic venue will host the Handball events.

Address: Anding Lu 1, Chaoyang District

Closest Subway Station: Olympic Sport Center Station

Transportation

Subway: Take subway No. 10 line, transfer at Xiongmao Huandao station, take the Olympic spur line (奥运支线) and then get off at Olympic Sport Center station.

Bus: Take any of the following bus such as 113，386，407，656，737，740，753，804，827，939，944，983; get off at bus stop Yayuncun.

Beijing Workers' Stadium (北京工人体育场)

Many of the most important football matches will be played at the home ground of Beijing Workers' Stadium.

The 72,000 capacity ground will also host the quarter-finals and semifinals of the 2008 Beijing Olympic football competition.

Address: Gongren Tiyuchang Bei Lu

Closest Subway Station: Dongsishitiao Station

Transportation

Subway: Take subway No. 2 line, get off at Dongsishitiao station.

Bus: Take any of the following bus such as 110，113，115，117，118，120，403，406，416，431，673，701，758，823; get off at bus stop Gongren Tiyuchang.

Beijing Workers' Gymnasium (北京工人体育馆)

Boxing and judo will be held in the 40,200 square meter Beijing Workers' Gymnasium. Built in 1961, it has hosted countless events over the years and has become an important center for sports. It has 12,000 permanent seats and 1000 temporary seats.

Address: Gongti Bei Lu, Chaoyang District

Closest Subway Station: Dongsishitiao Station

Transportation

Subway: Take subway No. 2 line, get off at Dongsishitiao station.

Bus: Take any of the following bus such as 110，113，115，117，118，120，403，406，416，431，673，701，758，823; get off at bus stop Gongren Tiyuchang.

Capital Indoor Stadium
(北京首都体育馆)

The Capital Indoor Stadium has a floor area of 54,600 square meters. It was built in 1968. The volleyball events will be held here for the 2008 Summer Olympics. This indoor venue has a seating capacity of 18,000 spectators.

Address: 54 Baishiqiao Lu, Xicheng District.

Closest Subway Station: Xizhimen Station

Transportation

Subway: Take subway No. 2 line or No. 13 line, get off at Xizhimen subway station

Bus: Take any of the following bus such as 104, 105, 106, 107, 111，114，118, 205，319，320, 332，334，347, 360，482，601, 632，634，645, 653，714，716，717，727，732，804，814，827 ; get off at bus stop Baishiqiao

Fengtai Sports Center Softball Field (北京丰台区丰台体育中心)

As the name suggests, Fengtai Sports Center Softball Field will host the 2008 Olympic softball competition. The venue has 15,570 square meters of floor space with 5,000 seats in the main stadium, 3,500 seats in the reserve stadium, and 5,000 temporary seats.

Address: 67 Fentai Chalukou, Fentai District

Closest Subway Station: Wukesong Station

Transportation

Subway: Take subway No. 1 line, get off at Wukesong station.

Bus: Take any of the following bus such as 310，313，338，351，657，804，958，996; get off at bus stop Fengtai Tiyu Zhongxin.

Yingdong Natatorium of National Olympic Sports Center （北京英东游泳馆）

Water Polo and the swimming discipline of the Modern Pentathlon will take place at the Yingdong Nataorium Olympic Sports Center which is located at 1 Anding Lu, Chaoyang District. The 44,635 square meter venue has some 6000 seats.

Address: Anding Lu 1, Chaoyang District

Closest Subway Station: Olympic Sport Center Station

Transportation

Subway: Take subway No. 10 line, transfer at Xiongmao Huandao station, take the Olympic spur line (奥运支线) and then get off at

Olympic Sport Center station.

Bus: Take any of the following bus such as 113，386，407，656，737，740，753，804，827，939，944，983; get off at bus stop Yayuncun.

Laoshan Mountain Bike Course （北京老山自行车馆）

Next to the Velodrome is the Laoshan Mountain Bike Course. The magnificent 6.2 kilometer 2008 Beijing Olympic course will hold 2000 spectators accommodated in temporary stands.

Address: 15 Laoshan Xi Lu, Shijingshan District

Closest Subway Station: Babaoshan Station

Transportation

Subway: Take subway No. 1 line, get off at Babaoshan station.

Bus: Take any of the following bus such as 325，327，337，354，385，389，472，621，622，663，728，941，958，959; get off at bus stop Jingyuanlukou.

Beijing Shooting Range Clay Target Field （北京射击场飞碟靶场）

Shooting events at the 2008 Olympics, including the men's and women's skeet shooting and trap shooting will take place at the Beijing Shooting Range Clay Target Field.

Address: Xiangshan Nan Lu Futianshi 3, Shijingshan District

Closest Subway Station: Pingguoyuan Station

Transportation

Subway: Take subway No. 1 line, get off at Pingguoyuan station.

Bus: Take any of the following bus such as 112，318, 347，489，664，992; get off at bus stop Beijing Shejichang.

Beijing Institute of Technology Gymnasium （北京理工大学体育馆）

The Beijing Institute of Technology Gymnasium, located in Haidian District in Beijing, will host the volleyball events for the 29th Summer Olympics.

Address: 5 Zhongguancun Nan Dajie

Closest Subway Station: Suzhoujie Station

Transportation

Subway: Take subway No. 10 line, get off at Suzhoujie station.

Bus: Take any of the following bus such as 205，320，332，653，716，717，732，804，808，814，827; get off at bus stop Nongkeyuan or Sanyimiao.

Beijing University of Aeronautics & Astronautics Gymnasium（北京航空航天大学体育馆）

An indoor arena in Beijing, built in 2000, the Beijing University of Aeronautics & Astronautics Gymnasium will host the weightlifting events for the 2008 Summer Olympics. Located in the Haidian District of Beijing, it can seat 5400 spectators.

Address: 37 Xueyuan Lu

Closest Subway Station: Zhichunlu Station

Transportation

Subway: Take subway No. 13 line, get off at Zhichunlu station.

Bus: Take any of the following bus such as 103，331，375，386，392，398，438，478，490，498，604，632，719，743，748，810，836，944; get off at bus stop Hangtian Hangkong Daxue.

Fencing Hall – National Conventional Center (国家会议中心击剑馆)

The fencing and modern pentathlon events for the 2008 Beijing Olympics will be held here. The preliminaries and finals of

the fencing events will be organized in the fencing gymnasium. The shooting discipline of the modern pentathlon will also be held in this gymnasium.

Address: Olympic Park

Closest Subway Station: Senlin Gongyuan Station

Transportation

Subway: Take subway No. 10 line, transfer at Xiongmao Huandao station, take the Olympic spur line (奥运支线) and then get off at Senlin Gongyuan station.

Bus: Take any of the following bus such as 109，305，315，333，344，355，392，407，419，478，490，604，618，670，719，748，752，753，810，819，839，909; get off at bus stop Qinghe Nanzhen.

Beijing Olympic Green Hockey Stadium (奥林匹克公园曲棍球场)

Beijing will host some of the hockey matches for the 29th summer Olympic Games at the temporary hockey field at the Olympic Green. The 11.87 hectare site can hold 17,000 spectators.

Address: Olympic
Park

Closest Subway
Station: Senlin
Gongyuan Station

Transportation

Subway: Take
subway No. 10
line, transfer
at Xiongmao
Huandao station,
take the Olympic
spur line (奥运支
线) and then get
off at Senlin Gongyuan station.

Bus: Take any of the following bus such as 109，305，315，333，344，
355，392，407，419，478，490，604，618，670，719，748，752，
753，810，819，839，909; get off at bus stop Qinghe Nanzhen.

Beijing Olympics Green Archery Field (北京奥林匹克公园射箭场)

The 2008 Olympic Archery
events will be held at the Beijing
Archery Field, which is located
at Olympic Green, Chaoyang
District. The 9.22 hectare field
can accommodate up to 5,000
spectators.

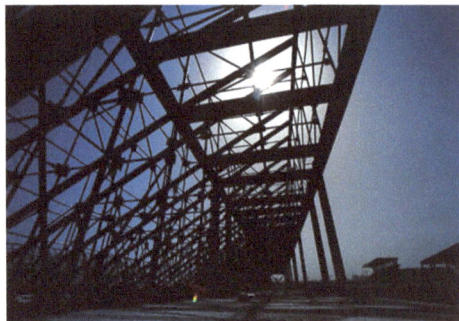

Beijing Wukesong Center of Baseball Field (北京五棵松棒球场)

The Summer Olympics 2008 baseball events will be held at Beijing's
Wukesong Center, Baseball Field. This 14,360 square meter venue can
handle up to 15000 spectators.

Address: Southwest corner in Wukesong Wenhua Tiyu Zhongxin

Closest Subway Station: Wukesong
Station

Transportation

Subway: Take subway No. 1 line, get
off at Wukesong station.

Bus: Take any of the following bus such as 115，337，370，373，436，620，624，654，711，728，740，748，751，804，817，840，913，952，967，982，983，996; get off at bus stop Wukesong.

Chaoyang Park Beach Volleyball Ground (朝阳公园沙滩排球场)

Beach Volleyball during the 29th Summer Olympics will take place in Beijing's Beach Volleyball Ground. It is located in Chaoyang Park in the Chaoyang District and has 12,000 seats for spectators.

Address: Chaoyang Gongyuan

Closest Subway Station: Gongti Beizhan Station

Transportation

Subway: Take subway No. 10 line, get off at Gongti Beizhan station.

Bus: Take any of the following bus such as 31，117，302，350，406，419，431，499，672，673，675，682，705，710，731，750，752，758，815，852，973，984，985，988; get off at bus stop Chaoyang Gongyuan.

Laoshan Bicycle Moto Cross (BMX) Field （北京老山小轮车赛场）

Built for the 2008 Beijing Summer Olympics, the BMX Field in Laoshan, Beijing will be the venue for the BMX cycling events.

Address: Laoshan, Shijingshanw District

Closest Subway Station: Babaoshan Station

Transportation

Subway: Take subway No. 1 line, get off at Babaoshan station.

Bus: Take any of the following bus such as 325，327，337，354，385，389，472，621，622，663，728，941，958，959; get off at bus stop Jingyuanlukou.

Triathlon Venue in Ming Tomb Reservoir (北京奥运会铁人三项)

The Olympic triathlon will take place at Ming Tomb Reservoir which is located in the District of Changping in the north of Beijing. This cost efficient venue will host swimming, running and cycling events and it covers approximately 11,767 square meters. Taking a taxi is the most convenient way to get there.

Address: Shisanling Shuiku

Road Cycling Course (城区公路自行车赛场)

Beijing's Olympic 2008 Urban Road Cycling Course will host the cycle race event. The course passes several Districts in Beijing, commencing at Yongding Men, and fishing at Juyongguan.

Non-Beijing Venues

Besides Olympic venues in Beijing, there are also venues in other cities in China. The rest of the venues are located in the following cities in China: Shanghai, Qingdao, Shenyang, Tianjin, Qinhuangdao and Hong Kong. In this book, we will cover all of the venues except those in Hong Kong.

Venue in Shanghai

Shanghai Stadium (上海体育场)

Built in 1997, the Shanghai Stadium is a multi-use stadium and can seat 80,000 spectators. It was ranked as the best sports architecture in Shanghai in 1998. The 2008 Beijing Olympic Games football preliminaries will take place in this190,000 square meter venue

which has seen many significant performance shows over the years.

Address: 666 Tianyaoqiao Lu, Shanghai City. Tel: (021) 64385200

Venue in Tianjin

Tianjin Olympic Center Stadium (天津奥体中心体育馆)

Another 2008 Beijing Olympic Games venue for football preliminaries is the Tianjin Olympic Center Stadium in Tianjin, China. This 78,000 square meter stadium measures 380 meters in length, 270 meters in width and 53 meters in height and has a capacity for 60,000 spectators.

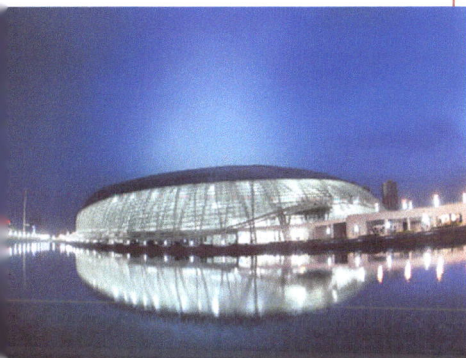

Address: Binshui Xi Dao, Hexi District, Tianjin City

Venue in Qinhuangdao

Qinhuangdao Olympic Sports Center Stadium （秦皇岛奥体中心）

2008 Beijing Olympic Games football preliminaries will also be played at the Qinhuangdao

Olympic Sports Center Stadium in Qinhuangdao. The multiuse stadium covers an area of 168,000 square meters and has a seating capacity of 32,572 of which 0.2% is reserved for disabled people.

Address: Hebei Dajie Xiduan, Haigang District, Qinhuangdao City

Tel: (0335) 8018018

Venue in Qingdao

Qingdao International Sailing Center （青岛国际航海中心）

Located in the city of Qingdao, Shandong Province in the east China, is the Qingdao International Sailing Center. This marina is the venue for the sailing events in the 2008 Beijing Olympic Games.

Originally the site was the Beihai Shipyard in Qingdao's Fushan Bay, but now this International sailing center covers an area of 45,000 square meters of which

two thirds will be used for the competitions.

Address: Fushanwan, Qingdao City

Venue in Shenyang

Shenyang Olympic Sports Center Stadium (沈阳奥体中心体育馆)

2008 Beijing Olympic Games football preliminaries will also be played at the Shenyang Olympic Sports Center Stadium which is a multiuse stadium in Shenyang. Built in 1989, the stadium has capacity for 65,000 spectators.

Address: Hunnan Xin District, Shenyang City

Sports Schedule

The following is the Olympic sports schedule for 2008 Beijing Olympic Games.

Event	Date	Venue
Opening Ceremony	August 8	Beijing National Stadium
Archery	August 9-15	Beijing Olympic Green Archery Field
Athletics	August 15-24	Beijing National Stadium
Badminton	August 9-17	Beijing University of Technology Gymnasium
Baseball	August 9-17	Beijing Wukesong Sports Center Baseball Field
Basketball	August 9-24	Beijing Olympic Basketball Gymnasium
Beach Volleyball	August 9-22	Chaoyang Park Beach Volleyball Ground
Boxing	August 9-24	Beijing Workers' Gymnasium

Canoe/Kayak—Flatwater	August 18-23	Shunyi Olympic Rowing-Canoeing Park
Canoe/Kayak—Slalom	August 11-14	Shunyi Olympic Rowing-Canoeing Park
Cycling—Track	August 15-19	Laoshan Velodrome
Cycling—Road	August 9,10,14	Road Cycling Course
Cycling—Mountain Bike	August 22-23	Laoshan Mountain Bike Course
Cycling—BMX	August 20-21	Laoshan Bicycle Moto Cross (BMX) Venue
Diving	August 10-13, 15-23	National Aquatics Center
Equestrian—Jumping	August 15,17,18, 21	Hong Kong Olympic Equestrian Venue (Shatin)
Equestrian—Dressage	August 13,14,16,19	Hong Kong Olympic Equestrian Venue (Shatin)
Equestrian—Eventing	August 9-12	Hong Kong Olympic Equestrian Venue (Shatin)
Fencing	August 9-17	Fencing Hall of National Convention Center
Football	August 6,7, 9-11, 12-13, 15-16, 18-19, 21-23	National Stadium, Beijing Workers' Stadium, Tianjin Olympic Center Stadium, Shanghai Stadium, Shenyang Olympic Stadium, Qinhuangdao Olympic Sports Center Stadium
Gymnastics—Artistic	August 9,10,12-15,17-19	National Indoor Stadium
Gymnastics—Trampoline	August 16,18,19	National Indoor Stadium
Gymnastics—Rhythmic	August 21-24	Beijing University of Technology Gymnasium
Handball	August 9-24	National Indoor Stadium
Hockey	August 10-23	Beijing Olympic Green Hockey Stadium
Judo	August 9-15	Beijing Science and Technology University Gymnasium

Modern Pentathlon	August 21-22	Olympic Sports Center Stadium, Yingdong Natatorium of National Olympic Sports Center, Fencing Hall of National Convention Center
Rowing	August 9-17	Shunyi Olympic Rowing-Canoeing Park
Sailing	August 9-21	Qingdao Olympic Sailing Center
Shooting	August 9-17	Beijing Shooting Range Hall, Beijing Shooting Range CTF
Swimming	August 9-17, 20,21	National Aquatics Center
Softball	August 12-21	Fengtai Sports Center Softball Field
Synchronized Swimming	August 18-20,22-23	National Aquatics Center
Table Tennis	August 13-23	Peking University Gymnasium
Taekwondo	August 20-24	Beijing Science and Technology University Gymnasium
Tennis	August 10-17	Beijing Olympic Green Tennis Court
Triathlon	August 18-19	Triathlon Venue
Volleyball	August 9-24	Capital Indoor Stadium, Beijing Institute of Technology Gymnasium
Wrestling—Greco-Roman	August 12-14	China Agricultural University Gymnasium
Wrestling—Freestyle	August 16,17,19-21	China Agricultural University Gymnasium
Water Polo	August 10-22, 24	Yingdong Natatorium of National Olympic Sports Center
Weightlifting	August 9-13, 15-19	Beijing University of Aeronautics & Astronautics Gymnasium
Closing Ceremony	August 24	National Stadium

3   ON ARRIVAL

From Airport to Hotel

Beijing is the main Olympic city for 2008 Olympic Games. Most of the Olympic Games will be held here. The People's Republic of China's capital, Beijing, is the first destination of most international visitors. For entry by flight into the People's Republic of China, Beijing Airport is the main destination point. Beijing Capital International Airport is Beijing Airport's official title.

In 1958, Beijing airport opened for commercial flights. This was the very first civilian airport on the Chinese mainland. There are currently 3 terminals to the Capital International Airport in Beijing. People refer to the terminals as Terminal 1, Terminal 2 and Terminal 3. The newest terminal, Terminal 3, is already in use. It is quite big. Several Chinese domestic commercial passenger air carriers utilize Beijing Capital International Airport as a hub. China Southern Airlines, Air China, and Hainan Airlines are just a few of the major airlines that offer regional service. Many regard the airport as one of the busiest in the world. While traveling to Chinese cities such as Hong Kong and Macau, many travelers from outside the country are routed via the Beijing. Beijing Capital International Airport offers regularly scheduled flights to Taiwan. You can also book a direct flight to Beijing from many airports in Europe and North America.

When traveling from the Beijing airport to the heart of the city please remember it is about 16 miles or 26 kilometers away, so take the travel time into consideration. To travel from airports to city centers, you may choose to take a taxi, shuttle or minibus. Taxi service is available in Beijing for a small fee. The cost to ride the airport shuttle from the Beijing Capital International Airport to the center of the city is approximately 16 Yuan RMB or $2 USD. The cost of a taxi ride will be about 80 Yuan RMB or $11 USD.

From Airport to Hotel

Communicating to Chinese People

"Chinese" covers a broad number of different languages, lumped into one language, with literally hundreds of different dialects in China. The official language is Mandarin Chinese, which is a northern dialect spoken by the people of Beijing. Most of the hotel staff knows how to speak English, so that is not a huge problem for travelers. However, it might be difficult to communicate if you're on the street. If you are planning to take a taxi, have someone write down the address of your destination in Chinese; this will hopefully eliminate any confusion.

Most young students have been studying English since they entered middle school. They will be eager and happy to help you if you have any problems. And besides, the citizens of Beijing are learning English. To offer a better service to international visitors, English speaking guides and volunteers are also on hand.

You will also find that the great English language newspaper "China Daily" (Monday to Saturday) is readily available in most hotels and newsagents. It is a rundown of national and international news. One popular source of information about things to do or see is the "Beijing Weekend", which comes out on Fridays. Hotel guests usually receive the "China Daily" for free; obtaining it in other places will cost you 1 Yuan. Copies of the quarterly newsletter "Welcome to Beijing" can be found the guest rooms of most four- and five-star hotels. There are various English language weekly and monthly "what's on" guides in Beijing with interesting features, restaurant reviews, classifieds, and more. Use one of these to discover information about exhibits, movies, plays, events, music, restaurants... They also include helpful information such as listings of dentists, tours, apartments for rent, etc.

The Chinese Language

The official language of the People's Republic of China is "Mandarin" (Putonghua). Mandarin is one of the hardest languages for Westerners to learn because of its character-based writing system and tonal nature. With the use of 5 Tones and limited number of sounds, words are formed. The tone with which a word is said can totally change the words meaning. Chinese people are typically impressed with people who make an effort to learn to speak their language, because it is very difficult. So they are generally forgiving of mistakes that you may make.

Pictograms were the basis from which Chinese script evolved. As long ago as 3,500 years ago, pictograms were utilized. These began as resemblances of the ancient Egyptian pictograms we are familiar with. Over time, the pictographs became increasingly abstract, although you can often see the links between the original pictogram and the modern character.

Lots of the characters are compounds of two or more smaller characters. Two or more characters make up the composition of some words. The meaning of multi-character words may be driven by the combined meanings or the combined sounds of the different characters. 2,000 characters will not encompass all the characters you should be familiar; however, you need to know at least this number to be considered proficient. Though the western eye would have trouble discerning it, mainland China uses a simplified version of the characters.

Chinese school children, as well as foreigners, learn Pinyin, an alphabet-based phonetic rendition of spoken Chinese used to help pronunciation. Pinyin allows non Chinese speakers to get the general idea of the sound of Chinese, and it also makes the words more recognizable and easily remembered by westerners. For this reason, you will most commonly see locations written in both Chinese and the Pinyin translation. Be aware that the older Chinese people are unable to read Pinyin.

Communicating to Chinese People

Foreign Currency Exchange

Chinese currency is called Renminbi, which means "people's money" and is abbreviated to RMB. The main unit of Renminbi is the Yuan, and the Yuan is broken down into Jiao and Fen. The conversion between the three looks like this:

1 Yuan = 10 Jiao =100 Fen

RMB can be found in both notes and coins. Paper notes are available in 100, 50, 20, 5, 2, and 1 Yuan; 5, 2, and 1, Jiao; and 5, 2, and 1 fen. Coin denominations are available in 1 Yuan; 5, 2, and 1 Jiao; and 5, 2, and 1 Fen. Smaller denomination like Yuan notes can be useful in payments for Taxis and other small payments Prices are constantly listed in Yuan.

They can be changed at international airports, main branches of the Bank of China and at major hotels, and offer a secure manner in which to carry money. Only guests are provided the service of exchanging money at any of the hotels. The exchange rate is set by the government, is usually better than cash, and is available for Australian, Canadian, US, UK, Japanese, and most western European currencies. In order to exchange any unused RMB at the end of your trip, you must save your currency exchange receipts.

ATM

You can find automated teller machines (ATMs) that accept cards with international logos (like Visa or American Express), and they allow you to display prompts in English. International cards are accepted at ATMs at branches of the Bank of China and the Commercial and Industrial Bank, as well as at some branches of other banks. Try to find machines with the symbols for international cards. Please be aware that although credit

cards are readily accepted at most hotels, they are usually not accepted in payment for train and air tickets.

You will be able to check your account without any trouble by using an Internet cafe or hotel business center, if you have an online banking account. There are service providers who can help you with money transfers, and the main Bank of China branches will do credit card cash advances for a 4% commission (weekdays 9am-4pm).

Foreign cards may be accepted by some other Beijing banks, such as HSBC and Citibank. There are not many of this type of ATM. It is very unlikely that you will be able to process overseas transactions at other internal Chinese banks. Chinese RMB currency is given out by the ATM machines discussed here. The cash will be removed from your foreign bank account. Usually, it will be converted to the currency of your country at a reasonable rate. Commission and transaction fees vary from bank to bank. If you are using an ATM / Debit card, usually the charges are comparable to drawing money in your own country (e.g. You will be charged the same $3 per transaction fee by Bank of America as you would at any other ATM in the United States.) If you decide to use your credit card, that will usually involve getting a cash advance on your credit, and this process can be very costly, depending on the rates at your bank and the speed at which you repay the money.

Below are some Bank of China branches in the Olympic cities in mainland China.

In Beijing, the Bank of China headquarter is located in 410 Fuchengmennei Dajie, phone: (010) 66016688. Bank of China Beijing Branch is located in 8 Yabao Lu, phone: (010) 65199114.

In Shanghai, Bank of China is located in 200 Mid. Yincheng Lu, Pudong New District. Tel: (021) 38824588.

In Qingdao, Bank of China is located in 59 XiangGang Zhong Lu. Tel: (0532)81858098.

In Qinhuangdao, Bank of China is located in 57 YingBin Lu. Tel: (0335)3619050

In Tianjin, Bank of China is located in 80 Jiefang Bei Lu, Heping District. Tel: (022)27102335.

In Shenyang, Bank of China is located in 253 Shifu Lu, Shenhe District. Tel: (024)22810556.

Credit Cards

In major tourist cities in China, the credit card is slowly achieving a higher acceptance rate. Master Card, Diners Club, JCB, and Visa are very useful cards to have. Most mid-range and high-end hotels (3 stars or higher) as well as Friendship Stores and some department stores will accept credit cards. Be aware that you must use cash not credit cards to pay for transportation, including flights. The Bank of China has made credit card advances quite common at their head branches. American Express has a representative office in 2101 China World Trade Center Shopping Arcade, 1 Jianguomenwai Dajie. Tel: (010) 65052888.

ON ARRIVAL

Lost or Stolen Credit Cards:

If you are a victim of theft, or simply lose your wallet, you should call all of your credit card companies as soon as possible. A police report number or record of the loss can be obtained from the Public Security Bureau, or police station. A majority of card companies provide an emergency toll free number, so that you can contact them if you lose your card, or if it gets stolen.

Credit Card Contact numbers in case of emergency are as follows:

Visa ☎ (010) 800-440-0027

American Express ☎ (010) 800-610-0277

Master Card ☎ (010) 800-110-7309

Diners Club ☎ (416)369-6313

Travelers Checks

Travelers Checks offer security and a more favorable exchange rate than cash in China. American Express checks, and those from major financial companies like Citibank, are accepted. Do take note, though, that you may have a problem if you try to use it in a store as opposed to a bank.

Carrying Money

The safest way to carry money is within a money belt or pocket stitched into your clothing. Using Velcro tabs to help seal your pockets is also a deterrent to thieves. It's always a good idea to leave some cash and records of your travelers' checks and passport numbers in your hotel room or other safe place, just in case something was to happen.

When a tourist is leaving China and wants to change his RMB back into dollars, he may have to present official exchange receipts. Reconversion is only allowed to be done upon departure

Map and Travel Guide

It is very helpful to get a city map. Generally, the city maps cost about 2 Yuan RMB each and are available at airports, news stands and railway stations. You can also buy English language maps from street vendors. In addition, make sure that you have an address card from your hotel so that you can show it to taxi drivers when you are ready to return.

Make sure your map is written in both Chinese and pinyin translations, so that both you and the local Chinese citizens will be able to read it.

You can buy the Beijing Tourist Map from hotel gift shops, newsstands, airport kiosks, or at the Foreign Languages Bookstore in the Wangfujung shopping District. Its address is 235 Wangfujing Dajie, Beijing. Tel: (010) 65126903. Another bookstore you may go to is the Friendship Store Bookstore. It is located in 17 Jianguomenwai Dajie. Tel: (010) 65003311.

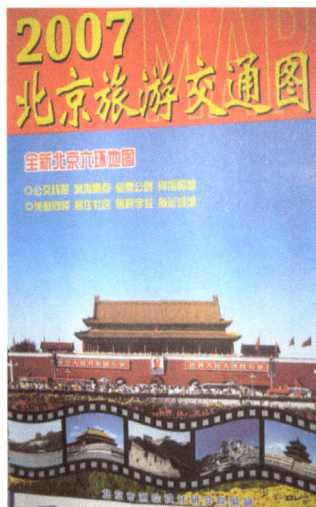

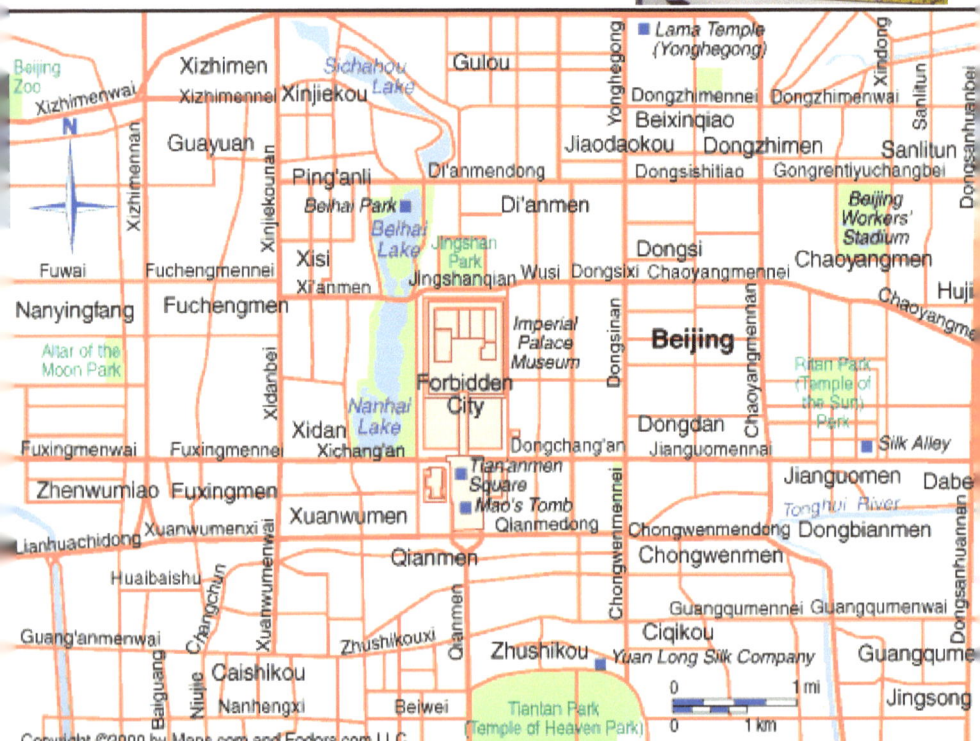

2007
北京旅游交通图

全新北京六环地图

Getting Around in Cities

T he difficulties of the past, associated with moving within China's cities, have nearly all been rectified. The best example of China's enhanced transportation systems can be found in Beijing. Beijing has spent tens of billions of dollars to improve the city's infrastructure, particularly transportation and housing, in preparation of the 2008 Olympic Summer Games. Even with these improvements, the sheer numbers of cars that people use today causes the city still seem to be very crowded. In the city you can travel by taxi, bus, minibus or subway, for rates that are much lower than those in the West.

If you are traveling on business, your host company will most likely arrange transportation for you, including airport pickups to and from meetings. If your host company will not be picking you up, you would be well served to take taxicabs and airplanes as your primary means of transportation. It helps to learn a few words and phrases in Chinese. Don't worry though, the differences in language is not that big an issue in today's world. Almost all service staffs speak at least a little bit of English. Additionally, the company's assistant or their interpreter will accompany you.

Plane

Domestic air travel is rapidly becoming the dominant mode of transportation for business travelers in China. Several airlines are based in the country and large airplanes can be accommodated at over 80 airports. The airline employees speak English and the service is equivalent to that of the United State air industry. All announcements are translated into English in airports and on planes. Cash payment is required for your airline tickets. You can find help arranging for tickets by contacting travel agencies, your hotel, or even a Chinese friend.

Train

Trains are a popular form of intercity transportation in China despite their crowded, uncomfortable, and dirty nature. Trains are a good option for traveling to cities without airports (like Tianjin) as rail lines connect all of the major cities.

When choosing seating, you have the option of a hard-seat, soft-seat, hard-sleeper, and soft-sleeper. Although the soft-seat and soft-sleeper train cars are more expensive, they include more privacy and legroom. The value of these benefits is immeasurable and worth the extra money if you are on a long trip, such as the well-traveled route between Shanghai and Beijing, which at its fastest is a 10 to 15 hour trip, and as long as a 40 hour trip on the slower trains. Soft-sleepers, going to the same destination, generally have ticket prices at a third to one half the price of domestic airlines.

Because seats on popular routes are snatched up fast, you should plan ahead and make your reservations early. Outlets for ticket purchases include: hotels, the internet, airline ticket counters and travel agencies. There is a fee for over 20 kilograms of luggage, which is the allotted amount. As part of the security process, remember luggage may be put through x-ray at many train stations. If you are unable to locate a suitable seat or bunk anywhere, you can usually pay a small fee to spend the night in the dining carriage - most overnight trains have them. Bringing food from home is recommended. The majority of the other people will be bringing items such as sausage, fruit or instant noodles. The train makes hot water available.

No matter where you want to go in China, not to mention most of Europe and Asia, taking the train is a popular choice.

Traveling from Beijing to Shanghai overnight usually takes approximately fourteen hours. Most trains leaving Beijing for major cities use the Beijing west station, but there is a second Beijing train station. The subway is the easiest way to get to the station. It should cost about 20-40 Yuan RMB to take a taxi from the Forbidden City. There is a ticketing office for foreigners in the station and most hotels can obtain tickets for you as well, although they may charge a fee. The largest rail terminal in Asia, Beijing's West Railway Station, is modern and well-equipped.

City Taxis

You can readily and cheaply hire a taxi in all major Chinese cities. You can expect to pay 2.00 Yuan RMB per kilometer for a taxicab in Beijing. It is not difficult to get a taxi on the street in a large city like Beijing because these days many taxis circulate throughout the city. Although, keep in mind that taxis cannot stop on occasional major roads where there are bans on stopping in certain locations, so getting one in these locations may prove difficult. You will find taxi cabs at the ready near large hotels, restaurants, train stations, buildings of businesses, as well as the airports. Cabs are readily available and reservations are not required. If you do reserve one, don't be surprised to find a surcharge on top of the general fee.

Be prepared for your taxi driver to have very poor English skills; however he will likely be very familiar with hotel and street names. A hotel card or written address of your destination should not be hard for them to understand. The Beijing Taxi Dispatch Center has a 24-hour dispatching service, its phone number is: (010) 68373399.

Usually taxis charge a base price of 10 Yuan RMB, or $1.25 USD for the first five kilometers. $$. 1.6 Yuan RMB (or 0.20 USD) is charged additionally per kilometer. You can find a price list posted on the rear side of the registered taxicabs. A meter will most likely be present in the cab to calculate your fare. After the driver turns the taximeter on, it will begin to indicate a baseline rate. It is not unusual for traffic jams to occur in larger cities like Beijing during rush hours (7:30 AM to 9:00 AM and 5:00 PM to 7:00 PM). If the taxi is stopped in traffic, an additional charge for minutes will be added to the mileage charge. Taking the taxi between the night hours, that is between 11.00 P.M. and 5:00 A.M., will result in 11 Yuan RMB (about 1.40 USD) being charged as a baseline. The mileage rate is also higher, but only a small percentage over the daytime rate.

When you get into the cab, be sure the meter has been turned off so you won't pay for other people's rides. Legally, the meter should be switched on at the beginning of your journey and off when you reach your destination. You can say "Qing Da Biao" if you find that the meter is not on. If you want to get off the taxi, you can say "Ting Che". If you need a receipt, ask the driver. It is always wise to keep a receipt as it minimizes the possibility of

being charged an unfair rate and it offers proof of expenditure so that you company can reimburse you. It is best to avoid confrontation if you are unfairly charged or receive bad service. If you'd like to register a complaint, call the pertinent authorities. You can find both the phone number and the cab number on your receipt. It is helpful to write down the taxi's license plate number in case you later need to file a complaint. People who travel on foot are in the most danger from Chinese traffic. As a pedestrian in China, travelers should be very wary on streets, especially at night.

When visiting China, there are several important rules of thumb regarding taxis. These rules include: avoiding unmarked taxis; knowing the approximate cost of your trip ahead of time; bringing written directions and your hotel's contact information; checking the meter before you depart; and using small bills for payment.

Rental Cars

Rental cars are available in some regions; however, this is not a recommended option for most business travelers. Driving accidents caused by aggressive drivers are common in China, where traffic rules are unclear and right-of-way etiquette is often overlooked. It's best to hire a driver if you rent a car, since the driver assumes all responsibility for damages to the car. In order to drive yourself, you must obtain an international driving permit from the American Automobile Association.

Subway

You will discover that the subway systems in Beijing, Shanghai, Tianjin, and Guangzhou are well developed and fairly easy to use. Subway stations, ticket booths, and transit points in these cities have their information posted in the Chinese and English language. The subway trains are scheduled to run from 5 am to midnight (05:00 and 24:00) at intervals of about every five minutes.

The quickest method to get from one place to another in

BEIJING Subway

▬▬▬	Line 1
▬▬▬	Line 2
▬▬▬	Line 5 *under construction*
▬▬▬	Line 13 City Rail

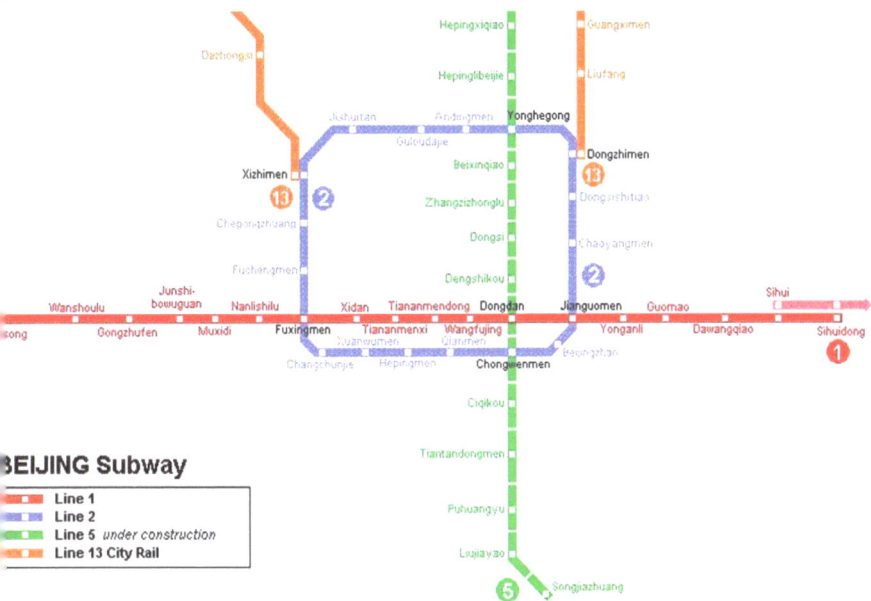

the center city area is by subway, although it is frequently crowded. Signs with a white capital D against a blue background are used to mark subway stations (from the pinyin word for subway, "ditie"). It makes no difference how far you travel over those routes; you will still pay the same fare.

Beijing subway system does not use the paper ticket anymore. It uses AFC system to automatically check your ticket. The ticket costs 2 Yuan RMB no matter where you go. It is better to use coins instead of paper money to buy the subway ticket. You can get 1 Yuan coin in the subway service counter and buy the ticket in the ticket machines. The AFC system is more efficient than the old paper ticket method.

Bus

In all the large cities of China the main mode of public transportation is still bus. City buses are usually very safe, and they'll be able to take you practically anywhere you'd like to get to. Bus travel is cheap, costing about a dime on the dollar. But the large size of the crowds congested traffic situations, and the routes that snake around can make bus travel an intimidating experience for foreigners. You won't be able to get much information about the places you are headed from bus drivers, because most of the do not speak English. If you decide to ride the buses, at the very least be sure to learn how to say the number of the route you want before you start out.

Buses in the city come in intervals of 5-to-10 minutes in between 5 a.m. and midnight. There are usually no more than two or three minutes between them during rush hour. You will most likely be pushed and shoved by the other people attempting to get on board, so be prepared. Tickets can be purchased from the conductor, and the charge will be dependent upon the number of stops on your bus route. Foreigners often find intercity buses crowded and hot (no air-conditioning), and they may be charged more than Chinese passengers. Regardless, if you plan to travel overnight, the bus is the least expensive way to do that.

Larger cities have more bus routes. The names of the buses generally corresponded with the route numbers: Route 1 is 1 Lu, Route 4 is 4 Lu, and Route 717 is 717 Lu. The Chinese word "Lu" means "route" in English. Most bus drivers do not speak English well, so if you plan to use the buses, you must be able to say the route number and your destination in Chinese. You will need to be able to explain where you are trying to go if you expect them to be able to provide any assistance.

There is more frequent service on bus routes in the inner city than on routes in the city outskirts. As an example, buses inside Beijing's third ring run from 5:00 in the morning until midnight and come in five-minute intervals. Outside of the fourth ring, buses come about every 15 minutes and cease operation at 8:30 pm. Buses come more frequently - every two to three minutes - during the rush hour.

Buses are a safer alternative of transportation in major cities given the challenging driving conditions; also they cover a large city area. Buses are a less expensive means of travel than taxis. Public buses cost 1 Yuan RMB (0.125 USD) to cover the first twelve stops; for each additional five stops 0.5 Yuan RMB (about 7 cents USD) is charged. The cost of a privately-run bus line is 1-2 Yuan RMB for the first ten stops, an additional ten stops costs 1 Yuan RMB.

But because there are so many passengers and the roads are so congested, foreigners often hesitate to ride the bus in China. Big groups of people have a tendency to congregate at the bus stops waiting anxiously to board. There is a lot of pushing and shoving during the boarding process. Intercity buses are not usually recommended for foreigners; the buses are extremely crowded and are not air conditioned. If you are willing to spend extra money, minibuses and some shuttle buses run between tourist attractions; they are air-conditioned and faster than intercity buses. These tickets cost 3-4 times more than the price of a regular bus ticket. It's possible to flag down a minibus by simply waving your hand, because there are not normally bus signs. Minibus drivers can let you off anywhere they are permitted to stop, making it a flexible travel option. Typical rush hours are from 6:30 to 8:30 am (06:30-08:30) and 5:00 to 7:00 pm (17:00-19:00).

As an alternative to the regular buses, minibuses and those buses which can be found in busy tourist locations are faster and offer an air-conditioned ride. Although the tickets are about three times as much as regular bus tickets, they are still less expensive than taxi fares. Bus stops are not the only places where you can get on and off a minibus; you can hail one by waving your hand and you can ask the driver to let you off anywhere along the route.

The Beijing bus system is excellent in the fact that it can get you almost anywhere you wish to go. But on the downside, the Beijing bus system buses are not very comfortable and tend to be extremely crowded. You can find modern, two-segmented gigantic buses that are air conditioned and very pleasant in the summer heat.

Which bus line to take to your destination? You can ask your hotel front desk. They are very familiar with the local area and can direct you to the right bus lines.

The four major bus stations with long distance service are as follows: Beijiao (north), Dongzhimen (northeast), Majuan (east), and Haihuhun (south). It is easier to get seats for a bus than a train if you are traveling to a city close to Beijing, such as Tianjin. If you are traveling a greater distance, you are better off taking the train.

Walk

You can certainly walk in the city to see daily life of ordinary Chinese people. Be aware that in major cities like Beijing, one block can be very long. You need a good walking shoe to walk. Use your map to find the destination and then try to locate the street sign when you are walking. The street names are written in Chinese characters and in Pinyin. There are some common elements in street names. For example, Bei in Pinyin means north. Lu in Pinyin means Road. So Bei Lu means North Road. Please refer to the common phrase list in the appendix to find more examples.

Transportation in other cities is similar as that in Beijing.

Get to Other Co-host Olympic Cities from Beijing

You can take the airplane to go to nearly Olympic co-host cities from Beijing. Here we give your some information if you want to go there using other transportation methods such as bus or train.

From Beijing to Tianjin

You can take bus from Beijing airport to Tianjin. You will arrive in front of the Friendship Hotel in Tianjin city. When you exit Beijing airport, you can go directly to the stand for buses to Tianjin. The ticket price is about 70 Yuan RMB.

Another way is to take the train. You can first take an airport bus or a taxi in the airport bus or taxi stand to Beijing Railway Station, and then take the train to Tianjin.

A new high-speed rail line between Beijing and Tianjin was completed in Nov, 2007. The starting station in Beijing is Beijing South Railway Station. Its speed is about 200 kilometers per hour and it will take 30 minutes from Beijing to Tianjin using this high-speed rail. It is an important project to serve the 2008 Olympic Games.

From Beijing to Shanghai

You can take a train. The Z train such as Z13, Z21, Z5, Z1 and Z7 will take you from Beijing Railway Station to Shanghai. To go to Beijing Railway Station, take an airport shuttle bus or a taxi.

In Shanghai, you can take subway line 1 and 2 to most of the scenic spots. You can also try to use the Maglev train; its speed is about 270 miles per hour. It will take only 8 minutes from Shanghai Pudong Airport to Longyang Lu subway station.

From Beijing to Qingdao

Regular trains T195 and T25 can take you from Beijing to Qingdao. It will take about 8 hours 30 minutes.

Starting from April 18, 2007, bullet trains are available to connect Beijing and Qingdao. The train will travel at about 200 kilometers per hour. It will take about 5 hours and 48 minutes to arrive in Qingdao. The Qingdao Shi Nan Train Station is closed for renovation for the 2008 Olympic Games and will be open in June 2008. Another train station in Qingdao is called Si Fang Train Station. It is near the Si Fang long distance bus station. The bullet train D51, D55 and D59 will take you from Beijing Railway Station to Si Fang Train Station. From Si Fang Train Station, you can take a taxi or bus to go to the destination you want to go to.

Getting Around in Cities

From Beijing to Qinhuangdao

Qinhuangdao is located about 320 kilometers north-east to Beijing. You can go to the Beijing Railway Station by subway (get off at the Beijing Zhan subway stop) or taxi first. Then take the train T509 to Qinhuangdao. In Qinhuangdao, there are train stations in Beidahe, Shanhaiguan and Qinhuangdao. Before you depart, ask to see if the train will stop at your ideal destination. From Qinhuangdao, it will take about 3 hours to Beijing, 4 hours to Tianjin and 5 hours to Shenyang by train.

If you want to take a bus, it will take 8-10 hours from Qinhuangdao to Beijing, 4 hours from Qinhuangdao to Tianjin. In Qinhuangdao, there are two long-distance bus stations. The Qinhuangdao long-distance bus station is located in Beihuan lu. The Beidaihe long-distance bus station is located in the intersection of Beining lu and Haining lu.

From Beijing to Shenyang

You can take train to Shenyang. The North Shenyang Railway Station is a railway station that can arrive at most cities in China, such as Beijing, Shanghai, etc. Tel: (024)62041168 or (024)22520858 or (024)22520878.

There are airport shuttle buses from Shenyang city to the airport. You may take the shuttle bus from an air tickets sales center located in Maluwan, 117 Zhonghua Lu. It will take about 40 minutes. Air Tickets Sales Service, Tel: (024)23197188

Shenyang Tiaoxian International Airport Tickets Sales Center, Tel: (024)24840445.

Telecommunications

Cell phone

If you are even able to use your mobile in China, you will probably be limited to making only calls to home, and it cannot be used to make local calls. So know your payment rates before you leave. It may save you money to use a readily available IP card to call home.

You can either bring your cell phone with you when you go to China or you can purchase one when you are there. A cheaper and more convenient way of communicating with your family and friends is by the use of a SIM card that you purchase locally and adding it to the phone. China has a network that is quite good, and signal should be good even in underground stores or other such areas.

A website sells GSM SIM cards. Its website is: http://www. gotobeijingchina.com. This SIM card allows you to upload unlimited photo and videos on your mobile phone to CBS iMobile. Their price is much lower than your cell phone's roaming fees. It is going to save you a lot of money. You can get more information from their website.

Telephone

You can make both international and domestic phone calls from your hotel room or from the hotel's business center. Long distance calls carry a 15% surcharge. International calls are not cheap. Reverse-charge calls do not cost as much as calling overseas from China, but the least expensive way to call home is with an IP card.

Mobile phones are ubiquitous in China, so you can easily purchase one to use and possibly even insert the card or chip from your own phone into your new phone. If you want to take home a phone that you purchased from China, be sure that it can handle the protocol standards of the country you live in. You will also be able to access email and whichever Internet instant messenger program you normally use.

Card phones

The easiest and most cost-effective way to make calls is utilizing widely available card phones. The IC Card is the first of the two types available, and it can be purchased in values of 20 Yuan and up and may be obtained from post offices, convenience store and street stalls. Most commonly, telephoning using one of these cards will cost between 0.30 and 0.50 Yuan, as long as it's not long-distance and not too long. The amount of money left on the card will be shown to you when you make a call, and there will be a countdown going while you are talking.

IP Cards

Rather than memorizing access numbers, you can make cheap international calls by using an IP (Internet Protocol) card wherever you see the letters IP. You can get about one hour of talk time with a 50 Yuan card depending where you are calling. The card has user instructions on the back: you dial the access number, choose the language from the menu, and dial in the number located behind the scratch-off panel.

Using a public telephone will necessitate an IC card which is required to make the first local phone call, as cash is not accepted. In the airport, there are IC card and IP cards on sale.

Placing Calls in and out of China

The international code to dial China is 86, and the local area code for the city of Beijing is 010. To make a call to China, some steps are to be followed: 1. Dial the international access code (for instance, 011 in the US, 00 in the UK); 2. Dial country code 86 for China; 3. Then dial the city code (like 010 for Beijing) omitting the leading zero; 4. Then dial the number.

For example, you would dial 00-86-10-XXXX-XXXX to reach Beijing from the UK. If your call is within the same city, do not dial the area code, which always starts with zero (for example: Beijing is 010 and Guangzhou is 020). From within your resort, you'll be able to make phone calls directly and to foreign destinations, but there may be a 15% fee for this service.

Non-local calls are still very cheap.

International calls can be placed from China by dialing 00, then the country code (U.S. or Canada 1, U.K. 44, Ireland 353, Australia 61, New Zealand 64). Then, dial the area or city code while omitting any leading zero, and proceed to dial the number.

Collect Call

For collect calls, dial 108; a Mandarin speaker may be needed to negotiate the call. Dial 114 if you would like to reach directory assistance. They do not speak English and they can only provide local numbers. Use the city code along with 114 to obtain numbers for other cities. If you need operator assistance, simply request help from your hotel.

Email/Fax

Email is the primary means of communication for most large companies. Numerous four and five star hotels provide high-speed internet connections in their centers for businesses, though they usually charge quite a bit. In some hotels, you can directly use your laptop to connect to internet using Wi-Fi. High-speed internet connections are available for a small fee from post offices, telecommunications offices, and internet cafes. Internet cafes are very popular, especially in university areas. Used more often than email, fax machines are available all over China. They're available in business-supply stores, and also probably in your hotel. Sending a fax in China costs the same amount as making a phone call, however hotels may tack on an extra 15 to 20 percent as a service fee.

Internet Access

Most of the hostels and hotels offer internet connection for a fee of 10 Yuan per hour. Beijing is host to a plentiful amount of Internet cafes (Wangba 网吧), almost all of which will get you connected in high-speed rather than dialup. In Beijing, you can find one famous internet café called Feiyu Internet Café (飞宇网吧) near the East Gate of The Central University of Nationalities, underground first floor. (中央民族大学东门飞宇网校地下一层) Tel: (010) 82615858. Bus: 332, 320,732, 727, 904, 921, 941, 827, 814, 804, 832, 808. Get off in Minzu Daxue(民族大学) bus stop.

Post Service

The desks at hotels typically supply Postal services. You can locate post offices near major tourist locations, train stations and main streets by finding the easily spotted green symbols, or you may be able to find post cards, stamps and mail boxes at a larger hotels. All seven days a week, from 9:00 to 17:00, you will find the post offices for business.

It costs 0.8 Yuan to send a letter within China, 2.5 Yuan to Hong Kong and Macao, and 5.4 Yuan to foreign countries. The International Post and Telecommunications Office handles regular postal services as well as remittances, money orders, telegraphic money orders, and domestic and international phone and telegraph needs. There is a Customs Office in the same building, in case you need to clear some items you are mailing. It is located in Yabao Lu, 300 meters northeast of Jianguomen. The phone number is (010) 65128132.

Couriers

Fedex office in Beijing is located in 32 Liangmaqiao Lu. Tel: (010) 64685566.

DHL office in Beijing is located in China World Trade Center, Room 111, 1 Jianguomenwai Dajie. Tel: (010) 65052173

4 OLYMPIC GAMES AND EVENTS

In this chapter, we will introduce many sport events which will be held in 2008 Summer Olympics. You can find information about your favorite games and its time and venue information. Then you can refer to chapter 2 to find more information about how to reach the venue to see your chosen games.

Opening Ceremony

The opening ceremony will be held in August 8 at 08:08:08pm in Beijing National Stadium in Beijing. Why so many 8s? That is because eight has special meaning in China. It means good luck and prosperity. During the opening ceremony, there will be fantastic performance shows, which are directed by Mr. Yimou Zhang, the famous movie director in China. The opening ceremony will demonstrate to the world a modern China by various performance shows.

Closing Ceremony

The closing ceremony will be held on August 24, 2008 in Beijing National Stadium. According to the assistant director for the opening and closing ceremonies of the Beijing 2008 Olympic Games, the closing ceremony would be the greatest in Olympic in history. This ceremony will be spectacular and memorable.

Aquatics

Women's swimming events have been a part of the Olympic Games since 1912. Nowadays, men and women each compete in 16 events. The program involves four different strokes across a range of distances. Swimming events in Olympics also include diving, synchronized swimming and water polo.

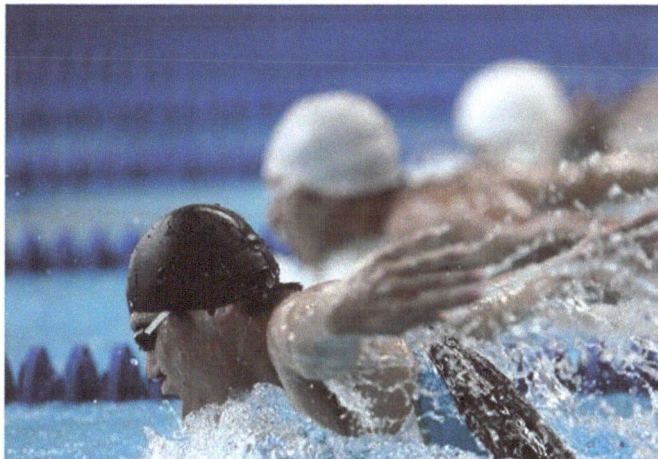

List of Events

100m backstroke Men, 100m breaststroke Men, 100m butterfly Men, 100m freestyle Men, 1500m freestyle Men, 200m backstroke Men, 200m breaststroke Men, 200m butterfly Men, 200m freestyle Men, 200m individual medley Men, 400m freestyle Men, 400m individual medley Men, 4x100m freestyle relay Men, 4x100m medley relay Men, 4x200m freestyle relay Men, 50m freestyle Men, marathon 10km Men, 100m backstroke Women, 100m breaststroke Women, 100m butterfly Women, 100m freestyle Women, 200m backstroke Women, 200m breaststroke Women, 200m butterfly Women, 200m freestyle Women, 200m individual medley Women, 400m freestyle Women, 400m individual medley Women, 4x100m freestyle relay Women, 4x100m medley relay Women, 4x200m freestyle relay Women, 50m freestyle Women, 800m freestyle Women and marathon 10km Women.

Diving: 3m springboard Men, synchronized diving 10m platform Men, synchronized diving 3m springboard Men, 10m platform Men, 10m platform Women, 3m springboard Women, synchronized diving 10m platform Women and synchronized diving 3m springboard Women.

Synchronized Swimming: Duet Women and team Women

Water polo: Water polo Men and water polo Women

Time and Venues

The swimming events will be held at the National Aquatics Center in the Olympic Green from August 9-24, 2008. The 10km marathon swimming event will be held at Shunyi Olympic Rowing-Canoeing Park on the side of Chaobai River in Shunyi District, Beijing.

Archery

Archery players can shoot the arrow at 240km per hour. This sport requires the player to have sharp eyes and steady hands.

List of Events

Individual (FITA Olympic round - 70m) Men, team (FITA Olympic round - 70m) Men, individual (FITA Olympic round - 70m) Women and team (FITA Olympic round - 70m) Women

Time and Venue

August 9-15, 2008 at the Olympic Green Archery Field

Athletics

Athletics is the oldest sport in all sports. It requires the athletes to be faster, higher and stronger. Nowadays, athletics is still one of the most popular Olympic sports.

List of Events

100m Men, 110m hurdles Men, 1500m Men, 200m Men, 20km walk Men, 3000m steeplechase Men, 400m Men, 400m hurdles Men, 4x100m relay Men, 4x400m relay Men, 5000m Men, 10000m Men, 50km walk Men, 800m Men, decathlon Men, discus throw Men, hammer throw Men, high

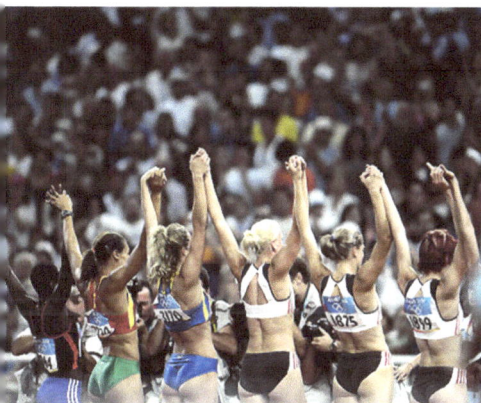

jumpx Men, javelin throw Men, long jump Men, marathon Men, pole vault Men, shot put Men, triple jump Men, 100m Women, 100m hurdles Women, 1500m Women, 200m Women, 20km race walk Women, 3000m steeplechase Women, 400m Women, 400m hurdles Women, 4x100m relay Women, 4x400m relay Women, 5000m Women, 10000m Women, 800m Women, discus throw Women, hammer throw Women, heptathlon Women, high jump Women, javelin throw Women, long jump Women, marathon Women, pole vault Women, shot put Women and triple jump Women.

Time and Events

August 15-24, 2008 at the National Stadium in the Olympic Green

Badminton

Badminton is a very popular sport in many countries. It became a competition sport at the Olympic Games in 1992. Badminton players need to run fast, react very quickly. During one match, one player could run over several kilometers. So it is a quite intensive game.

List of Events

Doubles Men, doubles Women, singles Men, singles Women, doubles Mixed

Time and venue

August 9-17, 2008 at the Beijing University of Technology Gymnasium

Baseball

Baseball is popular in many areas such as North America, Central America and Asia. It evolved from bat-and-ball games. At the end of nineteenth century, baseball was already recognized as the national sport in USA. The game is sometimes called hardball.

List of Events

Baseball Men

Time and venue

August 13-23, 2008 in the Wukesong Baseball Field in Beijing

Basketball

Basketball originated from USA. It was listed as the formal Olympic competition sport in 1936. The basketball was invented in USA in 1892. America is very strong in basketball games and has several strong basketball teams. The women basketball team in the Commonwealth of Independent States is very strong.

Chicago Bulls' Michael Jordan makes the winning shot during Game 6 of the NBA Finals against the Utah Jazz at the Delta Center in Salt Lake City, Utah, in this June 14, 1998 photo. AP Photo/Scott Cunningham
www.NBA.net

List of Events

(1) basketball Men

(2) basketball Women

Time and venue

August 9-24, 2008 at Wukesong Indoor Stadium in Beijing

Beach Volleyball

Beach volleyball is a team sport. Players play the game on sand. This sport is very popular in many coastal areas where there are sandy beaches. Beach volleyball became an official Olympic event in 1996.

List of Events

Beach volleyball Men and beach volleyball Women

Time and Venue

August 9-22, 2008 at the Chaoyang Park Beach Volleyball Ground

Boxing

Modern boxing originated from England. I was prevalent during the 17th century. Boxing was listed as a formal Olympic sport in 1904. Only the amateurs can participate in the Olympic boxing competition.

List of Events

+ 91kg (super heavyweight) Men, - 48kg (light-flyweight) Men, 48 - 51kg (flyweight) Men, 51 - 54kg (bantamweight) Men, 54 - 57kg (featherweight) Men, 57 - 60kg (lightweight) Men, 60 - 64 kg Men, 64 - 69 kg Men, 69 - 75 kg Men, 75 - 81kg (light-heavyweight) Men and 81 - 91kg (heavyweight) Men

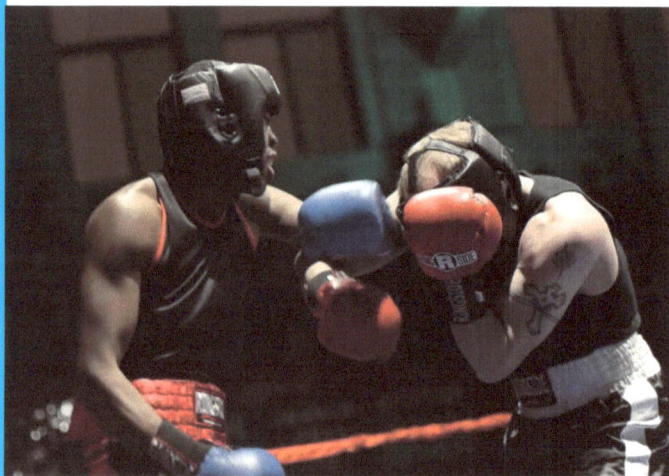

Time and venue

August 9-24, 2008 at the Workers' Indoor Arena in Beijing

Canoe-Kayak/ Flatwater

Canoe-kayak was a demonstration competition in the 1924 Olympic Games. It

become a full-medal sport in 1936. Europe is pretty strong in this Olympic sport.

List of Events

Canoe / Kayak Flatwater: C-1 1000m (canoe single) Men, C-1 500m (canoe single) Men, C-2 1000m (canoe double) Men, C-2 500m (canoe double) Men, K-1 1000m (kayak single) Men, K-1 500m (kayak single) Men, K-2 1000m (kayak double) Men, K-2 500m (kayak double) Men, K-4 1000m (kayak four) Men, K-1 500m (kayak single) Women, K-2 500m (kayak double) Women and K-4 500m (kayak four) Women

Canoe-Kayak/slalom

The sport became the formal Olympic sport in 1924. The whitewater version of canoe-kayak—slalom was introduced in 1972.

Canoe / Kayak Slalom:

C-1 (canoe single) Men, C-2 (canoe double) Men, K-1 (kayak single) Men and K-1 (kayak single) Women

Time and Venue

August 11-23, 2008 at the Shunyi Olympic Rowing-Canoeing Park on the side of Chaobai River in the Shunyi District of Beijing

Canoe-Kayak/slalom

Cycling

Many people can ride on bicycles. Bicycle is also one of the transportation tools in many countries. Quite some people use bicycle to do exercises in order to improve their health. There are four disciplines in the cycling completion: road, mountain biking, track and BMX.

List of Events

Cycling Road: individual road race Men, individual time trial Men, individual road race Women and individual time trial Women

Cycling BMX: Individual Men and individual Women

Cycling Track: Individual Pursuit Men, Keirin Men, Madison Men, Olympic Sprint Men, Points Race Men, Sprint individual Men, Team Pursuit (4000m) Men, individual pursuit Women, points race Women and sprint Women

Mountain Bike: cross-country Men and cross-country Women

Time and venues

The cycling events of the 29th Olympic Games will be held from

August 9-23, 2008. Track, mountain bike and BMX events will be held at Laoshan venues in Shijingshan District of Beijing. Road cycling will be held at the Urban Cycling Road Course.

Equestrian

Equestrian became a formal Olympic sport in 1900. There are 3 disciplines in the Olympic equestrian competition: Dressage, Jumping and Eventing.

List of Events

Equestrian / Dressage: individual Mixed and team Mixed

Equestrian / Eventing: individual Mixed and team Mixed

Equestrian / Jumping: individual Mixed and team Mixed

Time and venues

The equestrian events of the 29th Olympic Games will be held in Hong Kong, China from August 9-21, 2008. The jumping and dressage events will be held at the main venue in Shatin. The cross country competition will be held at Beas River.

Fencing

Originated from ancient combat, fencing became an Olympic sport in 1896. It was the first sport to allow professional players in the Olympic Games.

List of Events

épée individual Men, épée team Men, foil individual Men, sabre individual Men, sabre team Men, épée individual Women, foil individual Women, foil team Women, sabre individual Women, sabre team Women

Time and venue

August 9-17, 2008 at the Fencing Hall in the National Convention Center on the Olympic Green

Football

Football (or soccer game) became a formal Olympic sport in 1900. Football women was included in the Olympic family in 1996. There will be 12 women's teams and 16 men's teams in 2008 Beijing Olympic Games.

List of Events

Football Men and football Women

Time and Venue

August 6-23, 2008 in five cities, namely Beijing, Shanghai, Tianjin, Shenyang and Qinhuangdao

Gymnastics – Artistic

Artistic gymnastics is a sport that combines both aesthetics and athletics. It requires the players to be agile, strong and graceful.

List of Events

Floor exercises Men, horizontal bar Men, individual all-round Men, parallel bars Men, pommel horse Men, rings Men, team competition Men, vault Men, balance beam Women, floor exercises Women, individual all-round Women, team competition Women, uneven bars Women and vault Women

Time and venues

August 9-24, 2008 at the National Indoor Stadium

Gymnastics – Trampoline

Trampoline gymnastics was listed as one of the formal gymnastics disciplines in Olympic Games in 1999.

List of Events

Individual Men and Individual Women

Time and venues

August 9-24, 2008 at the National Indoor Stadium

Gymnastics – Rhythmic

Rhythmic gymnastics began as a sport in the 1940s in the Soviet Union. In 1961, it was recognized this discipline as a modern gymnastics.

List of Events

Group competition Women and Individual all-round Women

Time and venues

August 9-24, 2008 at the Beijing University of Technology Gymnasium

Handball

Handball is a sport that was first played by people in Germany at the end of 19th century. Men's handball became the Olympic sport at the 1936 Olympic Games. Women's

handball was listed as the official Olympic sport in 1976.

List of Events

Handball Men and handball Women

Time and Venue

August 9-24, 2008. The preliminary competitions will be held at Olympic Sports Center Gymnasium and the finals will be held at the National Indoor Stadium.

Hockey

In hockey game, players use sticks to hit a small ball. Hockey became an Olympic sport in 1908.

List of Events

Hockey Men and hockey Women

Time and venue

August 10-23, 2008 at the Olympic Green Hockey Field in Beijing

Judo

Judo is a Japanese martial art. In Judo, the player can throw the other player to the ground, choke him or subdue him by a maneuver. Men's Judo became an Olympic event in 1964. Women's Judo became an official event in 1992.

List of Events

+ 100kg (heavyweight) Men, - 60 kg (extra-lightweight) Men, 60 - 66kg (half-lightweight) Men, 66 - 73kg (lightweight) Men, 73 - 81kg (half-middleweight) Men, 81 - 90kg (middleweight) Men, 90 - 100kg (half-heavyweight) Men, + 78kg (heavyweight) Women, - 48kg (extra-lightweight) Women, 48 - 52kg (half-lightweight) Women, 52 - 57kg (lightweight) Women, 57 - 63kg (half-middleweight) Women, 63 - 70kg (middleweight) Women and 70 - 78kg (half-heavyweight) Women

Time and Venue

August 9-15, 2008 at the University of Science and Technology Beijing Gymnasium

Modern Pentathlon

Pentathlon is a sport that requires the player to show their endurance and flexibility. Modern pentathlon players can shoot, swim, jump and run to demonstrate their skills.

List of Events

Individual competition Men and individual competition Women

Time and Venue

Fencing and Shooting will be held in the Fencing Hall of National Convention Center at Olympic Green. Swimming will be held in the Yingdong Natatorium of National Olympic Sports Center. Running and Equestrian will be held in the Southern part of Olympic Sports Center.

Rowing

Rowing is a sport that can test the athletes' endurance. The athletes try to compete with other team on river or on the ocean. This sport is one of the oldest Olympic Games. It requires the crew to coordinate their effort very well.

List of Events

Coxless pair (2-) Men, double sculls (2x) Men, eight with coxswain (8+) Men, four without coxswain (4-) Men, lightweight coxless

four (4-) Men, lightweight double sculls (2x) Men, quadruple sculls without coxsw Men, single sculls (1x) Men, double sculls (2x) Women, eight with coxswain (8+) Women, lightweight double sculls (2x) Women, pair without coxswain (2-) Women, quadruple sculls without coxsw Women and single sculls (1x) Women.

Time and Venue

August 9-17, 2008 at Shunyi Olympic Rowing/Canoeing Park on the side of Chaobai River in Shunyi District, Beijing

Sailing

Sailing debuted in the Olympic Games in 1900. Women's sailing was added to the Olympic Games in 1988.

List of Events

470 - Two Person Dinghy Men, Laser - One Person Dinghy Men, RS:X - Windsurfer Men, Star - Keelboat Men, 470 - Two Person Dinghy Women, Laser Radial - One Person Dinghy Women, RS:X - Windsurfer Women, Yngling - Keelboat Women, 49er - Skiff Mixed, Finn - Heavyweight Dinghy Mixed and Tornado - Multihull Mixed

Time and Venue

August 9-21, 2008 at Qingdao Olympic Sailing Center

Shooting

Shooting sport can be traced back to ancient hunting activities. During shooting, the player needs to concentrate his attention on the small target in a noisy environment.

List of Events

10m air pistol (60 shots) Men, 10m air rifle (60 shots) Men, 25m rapid fire pistol (60 shots) Men, 50m pistol (60 shots) Men, 50m rifle 3 positions (3x40 sh Men, 50m rifle prone (60 shots) Men, double trap (150 targets) Men, skeet (125 targets) Men, trap (125 targets) Men, 10m air pistol (40 shots) Women, 10m air rifle (40 shots) Women, 25m pistol (30+30 shots) Women, 50m rifle 3 positions (3x20 shots) Women, skeet (75 targets) Women, trap (75 targets) Women

Time and Venue

August 9-17, 2008 at Beijing Shooting Range Hall and Beijing Shooting Range CTF at Shijingshan District in Beijing

Softball

Softball is not really soft. It is nearly hard as a baseball. A very good player can throw the softball at about 99 miles per hour, which is very fast. It requires the players to react very quickly.

List of Events

Softball Women

Time and venue

August 12-21, 2008 at Fengtai Softball Field in Beijing

Table Tennis

Table tennis originated from England. It became an official Olympic sport in the 24th Olympic Games in 1988. In China, table tennis is very popular. There are about 40 million players in the whole world.

List of Events

Singles Men, team Men, singles Women and team Women

Time and Venue

August 17- 31, 2008 in the Peking University Gymnasium

Taekwondo

Taekwondo is a kind of Korean martial art. Two players can attach each other using their hands and feet. Taekwondo is a very popular sport in South Korea. It became the official Olympic sport in Sydney Olympic Games.

List of Events

+ 80 kg Men, - 58 kg Men, 58 - 68 kg Men, 68 - 80 kg Men, + 67 kg Women, - 49 kg Women, 49 - 57 kg Women and 57 - 67 kg Women

Time and Venue

August 20-23, 2008 at University of Science and Technology Beijing Gymnasium

Taekwondo

Tennis

Men's tennis became an official Olympic sport in 1896. Women's tennis was include in the Olympic sports family in 1900. Because it was hard to distinguish between professional players and amateurs, the tennis sport was once dropped from the Olympic sports family. In 1988, it returned to Olympics again as a medal sport. Tennis sport in Olympic

Games consists of men's and women's singles and men's and women's doubles.

List of Events

Doubles Men, singles Men, doubles Women and singles Women

Time and venue

August 10-17, 2008 at the Olympic Green Tennis Center in Beijing

Triathlon

The triathlon sport includes 3 disciplines: cycling, running and swimming. It requires the player to have very intensive training to excel in 3 different disciplines.

List of Events

Individual Men and individual Women

Time and Venue

August 18-19, 2008 at a scenic area of the Ming Tomb Reservoir in Changping District of northern Beijing

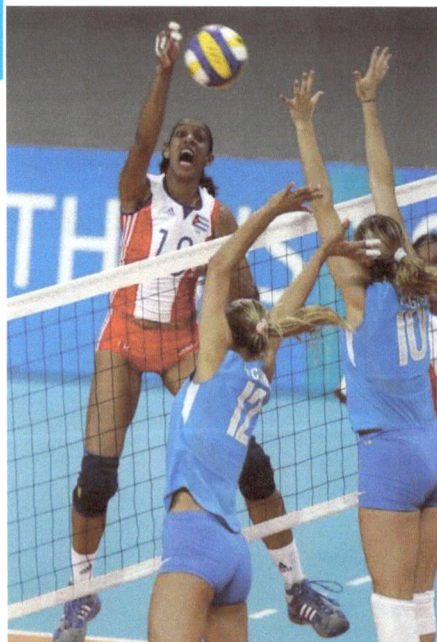

Volleyball

Volleyball is a team sport. It includes 12 players, with 6 players on each side of a high net. One team tries to hit the volleyball onto the ground of another team's court. Volleyball debuted in the Olympic Games in 1964.

List of Events

Volleyball Men and volleyball Women

Time and Venue

August 9-24, 2008. The preliminary competitions will be held at the Capital Indoor Stadium and Beijing Institute of Technology Gymnasium and the finals will be held at the Capital Indoor Stadium.

Weightlifting

In the old days, people lifted heavy stones to show their strength. This is the origin of the weightlifting sport. Men's weightlifting became an Olympic sport in the first modern Olympic Games in 1896. In 1920, it became a fixed competition sport. Women's weightlifting debuted in the Olympic Games in 2000.

List of Events

+105kg Men, 105kg Men, 56kg Men, 62kg Men, 69kg Men, 77kg Men, 85kg Men, 94kg Men, +75kg Women, 48kg Women, 53kg Women, 58kg Women, 63kg Women, 69kg Women and 75kg Women

Time and Venue

August 9-19, 2008 at Beijing University of Aeronautics & Astronautics Gymnasium

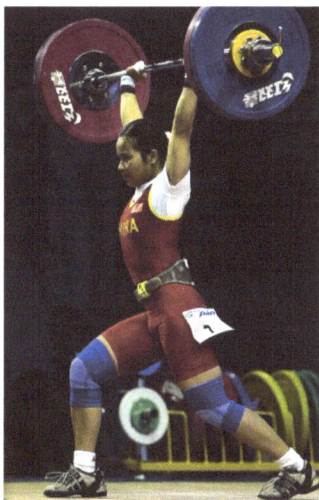

Wrestling

As one of the oldest sports in the world, wresting has attracted many people's interests. Originally, players can only use their arms and upper bodies to fight. Later, "freestyle" wresting was introduced and a player ca n use his leg to push, trip and lift his opponent.

List of Events

Wrestling Freestyle: - 55kg Men, 55 - 60kg Men, 60 - 66kg Men, 66 - 74kg Men, 74 - 84kg Men, 84 - 96kg Men, 96 - 120kg Men, - 48kg Women, 48 - 55kg Women, 55 - 63kg Women and 63 - 72kg Women

Wrestling Greco-Roman: - 55kg Men, 55 - 60kg Men, 60 - 66kg Men, 66 - 74kg Men, 74 - 84kg Men, 84 - 96kg Men and 96 - 120kg Men

Time and Venue

August 12-21, 2008 at China Agriculture University Gymnasium in Beijing

5 SIGHTSEEING IN OLYMPIC CITIES

Besides above Olympic venues, we are sure that you want to visit many beautiful travel attractions during your stay in the Olympic co-host cities in China. Here we give you some ideas about where to go in these Olympic cities in mainland China. We will cover famous travel scenic spots in Beijing, Shanghai, Tianjin, Shenyang, Qinhuangdao and Qingdao.

Beijing

The pride of China is encapsulated in its modern Olympic capital city; Beijing is a fashionable tourist destination which is becoming ever more popular for many reasons. Beijing is a fascinating city; the modern political, cultural and educational center of China is also the center of a number of key historical events. Beijing is a sightseer's paradise. Every year thousands of visitors are attracted to its famous historic sites and temples. The world famous Great Wall of China is only a bus ride away and a definite must-see. Beijing's major attractions include:

Tiananmen Square (天安门广场)

Chairman Mao, the first Communist Party leader founded the People's Republic of China here on October 1, 1949. This 400,000 square meter, key historic center is located in the heart of Beijing. Every year thousands visit Mao's remains in the mausoleum, the Great Hall of the people [National People's Congress] and gaze at the 15th Century Qianmen City Gate, which at one time protected the ancient inner city.

Address: Tiananmen Dong

Subway: Tiananmen Dong Station

Tel: (010) 65243322

The Forbidden City (故宫)

Home to the imperial household, this 720,000 square meter early 15th century site was built by Emperor Yongle. It was the imperial palaces of the Ming and Qing dynasties with 14 Ming and 10 Qing dynasties ruling from 'the Palace Museum' as it was known. The site's 800 buildings with its 9999.5 rooms are in good condition. The Forbidden City, ancient China's largest architectural area still standing, largely has its original layout but has been enlarged several times. The Forbidden City had some expensive renovation work after liberation and the Chinese government listed it as 'one of the most important historical monuments under special preservation'.

Address: Tiananmen Dong

Subway: Tiananmen Dong Station

Tel: (010) 65132255

Lama Temple (雍和宫)

Lama Temple was built in 1694 as the residence of the Emperor Yongzheng and it was transformed into a Buddhist temple in the mid 18th century. In the temple's teaching and assembly hall 'The Falun Dian', there is a large bronze statue of Tsongkapa, the founder of the Buddhist Yellow Hat sect.

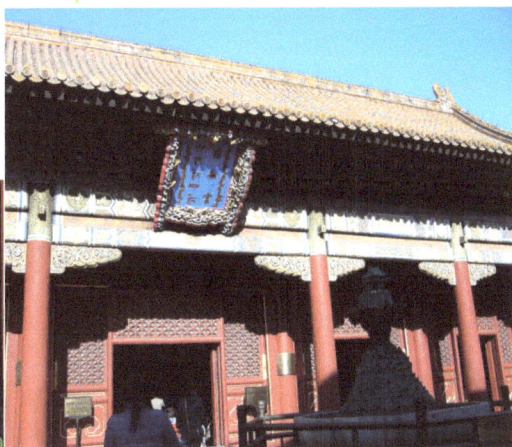

Beijing

Address: 12 Yonghe Gong Dajie

Subway: Yonghe Gong/Lama Temple Station

Tel: (010) 64044499

Summer Palace (颐和园)

The Summer Palace is located approximately 20 km north-west of Beijing's center. It is the biggest and best preserved imperial garden in China today. Kunming Lake and Longevity Hill are very famous. As with most imperial palaces, it is divided into three parts: the living quarters, the religious buildings and the halls for political affairs. The Summer Palace's important structures are: the Painting Walkway, which is the longest walkway in the gardens with over 14,000 traditional paintings on the beams and crossbeams and Empress Dowager Ci Xi's 50th birthday present, the Marble Boat in which she could take pleasure from the lake's hazy panorama during rainy days.

The imperial family would use the Summer Palace to relax and to get away from their buy life. A range of buildings and gardens grace the grounds, these including the Hall of Benevolence and Longevity and the spectacular Fragrant Buddha Tower with its wonderful view of Kunming Lake.

Address: Yiheyuan Lu

Subway: Wudaokou Station

Tel: (010) 62881144

The Great Wall

There is no doubt that the great wall of China is one of the world's places of interest, it is an amazing ancient construction reaching more than 5,000 kilometers and can be seen from space. A good place to see the wall near Beijing is Badaling in Yanqing County, which is located around seventy kilometers from Beijing.

Take the Tourist Buses from Qianmen Station or Bus 919 which departs from Deshengmen Station.

Tel: (010) 69122222

Factory 798

This 1950s concrete factory is now a well-known arts center featuring photographic exhibitions, video installations and other art works.

UCCA or Ullens Center for Contemporary Art, a rare non-profit arts organization, boasts Bauhaus-style with 9.5m high ceilings and exposed support beams in this ex electronics factory. In the 1990s Beijing's northeastern Dashanzi

Website: http://www.ullens-center. org

Temple Of Heaven (天坛)

Constructed in the early 15th century, this vast park contains several fascinating structures. A carved stone stairway which leads to the entrance of the Hall of Prayer for Good Harvests can be found in the north of the park. It has a cylindrical blue tiled roof with a stunning decorated ceiling.

Address: Tiantan Donglu

Subway: Qianmen Station

Tel: (010) 67028866

neighborhood 798 art District came into being with the conversion of massive factories into galleries and cafés. There are numerous studios, book shops and restaurants there.

Address: 798 art District, 4 Jiuxianqiao Lu

Subway: Dongzhimen Station

Tel: (010) 84599269

Hutong Tour by Pedicab

A pedicab guide, traditionally dressed, will take you into these Beijing Hutongs and tell you the history of the courtyards while you on the pedicab. If you go there alone, you are unlikely to find many interesting places or learn the history of the areas.

As there are several different routes for Hutong tours you may visit private homes in old traditional courtyards, have tea or dinner and chat with the hosts, visit the local. It is called "Being a Beijing person for one day". Make sure you negotiate the price first before you take a pedicab. Tours start from about 100 meters west of the north gate of Beihai Park.

Beijing

Capital Museum

Beijing Capital Museum has magnificent architecture, a lot of exhibitions, advanced technology and complete functions. It is very large and modern, and ranks among

首都博物馆

the first class museums in the world.

Add: 16 Fuxingmenwai Dajie, Xicheng District

Subway: Muxidi Station

Tel: (010) 63370491

Website: http://www. capitalmuseum.org.cn

Bell Tower and Drum Tower

North of the Forbidden City is the historic Dongcheng District. Just east of Qianhai Lake in the northwest corner of this District are two towers dating from the 13th century. A little to the south, after climbing the steep steps, the Drum Tower gives an elevated view of the traditional hutongs with their narrow residential alleyways which surround the Forbidden City.

Address: Dianmenwai Dajie

Subway: Gulou Dajie Station

Tel: (010) 64012674

Shanghai

Shanghai is the largest port and economic trade center in China with a comprehensive industrial base. It is a municipality under the direct jurisdiction of the Central Government. Shanghai is known the world over for its prosperity, cosmopolitan character and its wealth of human resources. After successfully winning the bid to host World Expo 2010, Shanghai is becoming more attractive and exciting, attracting people from all over the world. Shanghai's major travel attractions include:

The Bund (外滩)

Shanghai's modern history is epitomized by The Bund. This elegant multilane highway divides the historic side with its 52 glorious blocks of varying architectural styles built between 1870s and 1930s. On the other side, bustling crowds of visitors stroll along its wide embankment and feast their eyes on the breathtaking urban scenery of Shanghai and its Huangpu River. It is wonderful to cruise the Huangpu River to experience its beautiful scenery.

Yu Yuan Garden (豫园)

Appetizing food and tourist souvenirs can be found here in many restaurants and shops. Dragon Wall, the vast rockery, the Huxinting Teahouse and City God Temple are all worth a visit. The maze like 'Old Street' of Shanghai is like a magnet for travelers from around the world.

Address: 269 Fangbang Zhong Lu (Shanghai Old Street).

Shanghai

Chenghuangmiao (城隍庙)

Shanghai Nanxiang small steamed dumplings are available here along with a large range of traditional foods and Shanghai snacks. In this area traditional and fashion shops can also be found, alone with souvenirs outlets. Chinese and foreign tourists are attracted by the Chenghuangmiao architecture and the local atmosphere.

Xintiandi (新天地)

Xintiandi or New Territory is where "yesterday meets tomorrow in Shanghai today". Shanghai Xintiandi is a new Shanghai landmark where local people and visitors from other parts of China, along with foreign tourists, are enjoying the city's magnificent transformation into a thriving international metropolis.

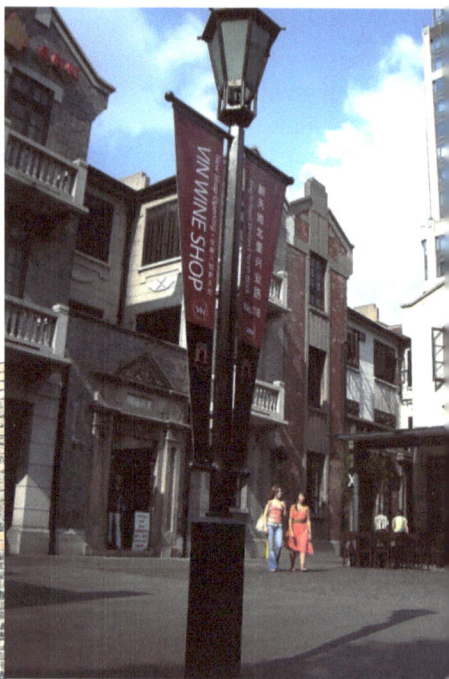

Jinmao Tower (金茂大厦)

Jinmao Tower is an 88-story, 421 m building. It is one of the tallest buildings in China and in the world. There is a food court in the basement. From the top floor you can see the whole Shanghai from a different perspective. It is located in 88 Shiji Dadao. The closest subway station is Lujiazui Station. Tel: (021) 50475101.

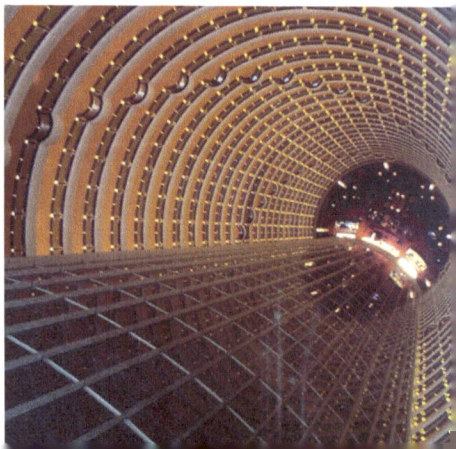

Tianjin

Only about one hours train ride from Beijing is Tianjin with its refreshing sea air. Enjoy the sea breeze and view the sights of the Chinese revolution along with historical relics, temples, churches and beautiful natural scenery.

Dule Temple（独乐寺）

A complex of grand structures more than 1000 years old, Dule Temple also boasts China's oldest multistoried wooden pavilion. Also to be seen is the Kwan-yin statue, which is one of China's biggest clay sculptures surviving today.

Website: http://www.dulesi.com/

Water Park (水上公园)

Arched bridges and small mounds connect the twelve small islands. Lotus flowers bathing in the water and weeping willows along the water's edge create a relaxing environment for your visit. In the south of the park, there is a zoo which contains many rare animals. You can take bus line 16、94、98、8、611、612、848 to get there.

Panshan Mountain (盘山风景区)

It is one of Tianjin's famous attractions. You will be happy to see unusual rock formations, grand peaks, clear stream lakes, and many verdant trees. Shang Pan, Zhong Pan and Xia Pan make up its three areas, famous for its vigorous pine trees, unique rocks and crystal clear stream water respectively.

Tianjin TV & Radio Tower (天津广播电视塔)

Located in Tianta Lake, Tianjin TV and radio tower is the fourth highest in the world. Bird's eye view dining takes place in the hanging restaurant at a height of 248 meters to 278 meters and can provide over 200 guests at a time with a memorable dining experience. A visit costs 50 Yuan. You can take bus line 8、9、16、94、98、161、168、178 to go there.

Qinhuangdao

The all-weather port of Qinhuangdao is a beautiful coastal resort in northern China. Its number one visitor attraction has to be the Great Wall and the seashore, but the historical Shanhaiguan Pass and the magnificent summer holiday resort of Beidaihe with its abundant tourist resources such as forests, mountains, lakes, rivers, springs, beaches, temples, gardens, harbors and ancient passes also attract many visitors.

Shanhaiguan (山海关)

Encircling walls linked to the Great Wall form an enclosed area. Laolongtou or Old Dragon's Head is at the east end of the Great Wall. The first Pass of great military importance located in the center of the town, is Shanhaiguan Pass or First Pass under Heaven.

diving club. Carnival activities are often held there.

Beidaihe Scenic Spot (北戴河景区)

With its beautiful long coastline, soft beach, and seaside attractions, Beidaihe is a popular sunbath and swimming summer resort. It is a first-class destination for travelers.

Shanhaiguan Great Wall Museum is north of Jingbian Tower and provides a detailed history of this world monument. You can take bus No.23 from the Mengjiangnu Temple to the Shanhaiguan.

Ledao (Shanhaiguan Happy Ocean Park) is located 2 km (1.2 miles) west of Laolongtou and is the largest shark aquarium in China. It is also northern China's largest

Nandaihe Tourist Resort （南戴河景区）

A bridge connects Nandaihe with its neighboring summer resort of Beidaihe [Funing County]. Soft sand, blue skies, fresh air and sunshine make Nandaihe one of China's top seaside resorts. Crossing over the sea by cableway, many exciting activities can be found at Xianluo Island amusement park. Bungee jumping, a sightseeing tower and other activities are on offer here. Nandaihe International Recreation Center in a forested area of Nandaihe and Nandaihe Water Park on the south side of Huanhai Lu may also interest the visitors. You can take bus No.22 from the Beidaihe Railway Station to Nandaihe Tourist Resort.

Qingdao

A picturesque red roofed city on the south coast of the Shandong Peninsula, Qingdao is a popular holiday and health resort due to its mild climate, bathing beaches and Mount Laoshan. It is especially popular in summer when visitors want to escape the heat of the cities. Each year, a lot of domestic and foreign visitors come to Qingdao to enjoy their vacation.

It is similar as California in USA in some way.

Qingdao is a famous industrial city and a major foreign trade port. The famous refrigerator company Hai'er and TV Company Hisense are located in Qingdao. Its mineral water, wine, and excellent Tsingtao Beer are world-famous. Shell carvings are very popular with tourists.

The Qingdao pier (青岛栈桥)

Constructed during the Qing Dynasty in 1890, in the reign of

Emperor Guang Xu; this pier has become a symbol of the city. It is four hundred meters long and ten meters wide, ending in a colorful two-story octagonal structure called Huilange or Wave Stopping Pavilion.

Lu Xun Park (鲁迅公园)

Adjacent to the No. 1 bathing beach, this great picnic spot with a view of the ocean used to be known as Seaside Park. 'A fairyland by the sea' was how Li Bai, a famous poet of the Tang Dynasty described it. "Wonderland on the Sea" is still inscribed on the park's memorial archway. An aquarium, an aquatic museum and a big seal pool are some of the park's attractions.

Laoshan Mountain (崂山)

Mount Laoshan grandly rises from the sea with extraordinary rock formations and sheer cliffs. It is located twenty kilometres east of Qingdao in the south of the Shandong Peninsula. Trees and grassland thrive on the mountain due to its plentiful rainfall. There are temples in Laoshan, if you are interested in Taoism; these temples are worth a visit.

Qingdao

Badaguan Scenic Area (八大关景区)

Located in the east of Qingdao City, is a famous scenic area called Badaguan. It means 'eight passes' as there used to be eight avenues named after eight famous passes in China. Today there are actually ten avenues as two more have been added since 1949. They are near the ocean with many trees, quiet streets and beautiful buildings.

Walking Tour in Qingdao

Modern Qingdao must-see scenic spots include 54 square, located near the Qingdao City Government in Xianggang Zhong Lu. Another nice pubic square is called Huiquan Square, located very close to the No. 1 Ocean Beach, in Nanhai Road. Closest hotel to the Huiquan Square include Huanghai Hotel, Huiquan Dynasty Hotel.

You can first go to Qingdao Pier, then go to Luxun park. From Luxun Park, you can see the No. 1 Ocean Beach. Huiquan Square is nearby. Not far away from the Huiquan Square, you will find the Badaguan Scenic Area. To go to 54 square, you can take a bus from Zhong Shan Park station. To go to Laoshan Mountain, you probably will need to take a taxi since it is a little far from the downtown Qingdao.

Shenyang

One of the earliest cities to be called a tourist city in China is Shenyang. This was due to its historical and cultural importance. There are over 1,100 relics and historical sites, above and below ground and 200 natural scenic spots to see. Shenyang four distinctive seasons; the mountains and rivers encircle this thriving and attractive city.

Shenyang Botanical Garden (沈阳植物园)

Covering an area of 189 hectares (467 acres), the Garden specializes in showing various kinds of plants from China's Northeast, North, Northwest and Inner Mongolia. It is an all the year round attraction but many people choose to go there in the summer to admire the large number of species of plant, the waterfall and the lake. With over 1,700 kinds of plants, it has become a tourist attraction. Visitors may also play golf in the garden. Entry ticket is 20 Yuan per person. You can arrive there by bus No. 234 from Dongling station and then get off at Zhiwuyuan bus station.

The Shenyang Imperial Palace (沈阳故宫)

China's only other royal palace outside of Beijing's Forbidden City and covering only one twelfth of its area, The Shenyang Imperial Palace is located at No. 171, Shenyang Road, Shenhe District in Shenyang City. The palace covers an area of over 60,000 square meters; the main structure was built in 1625 when Nurhachi ruled. More than three hundred rooms form twenty courtyards within its structure.

Liaoning Provincial Museum (辽宁省博物馆)

A first-rate museum, located at No. 26 Shiwei Road, features many relics of China's past and a few examples of modern art. A great place to gain a perspective on China's five thousand years of history.

6 FOOD AND ENTERTAINMENT

Chinese food enjoys a good reputation. You may have already experienced Chinese food in restaurants in the western cities. In China, you will see a vast array of Chinese dishes. In general, the range and quality of food found in China is much better than that found in western Chinese restaurants. Here we will introduce the traditional Chinese food to you and show you where to find the gourmet areas with numerous restaurants. Additionally, western restaurants such as Pizza Hut, Starbuck's McDonalds, etc are also covered in this guide. There are also many bars in these Olympic cities where you can relax a little bit.

Traditional Chinese Food

Beijing

Beijing must rank as an international city in terms of its culinary offerings, local people and visitors can try dishes from across China and around the world. Different kinds of restaurants are located almost everywhere in Beijing, most of its hotels offer both Chinese and western food.

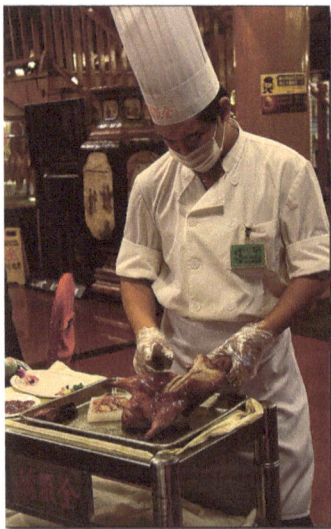

The regional cuisine usually consists of foods cooked by frying, stewing, roasting, braising and steaming. A famous example of Beijing cuisine is Beijing Roast Duck, along with Shuanyangrou or "Hot Pot", which are popular during the cold winter season. Arguably, the supreme cuisine is from the Imperial kitchen.

In western culture, each person has their individual plate, whereas in Chinese culture the food is placed in the center of the table, and shared by everyone. The Chinese people are very friendly and

generous. If you are the guest of a Chinese host, expect to be offered copious amounts of food, as Chinese culture dictates.

Usually when drinking beer, wine or spirits with Chinese, they will say "Gan Bei" which means bottoms up or cheers. Other than beer, the most popular Chinese alcoholic drink is a high-proof white spirit called Bai Jiu which is made from assorted grains. The degree of Bai Jiu varies, there is a Beijing brand called Erguotou which contains 56% alcohol. Compare to Erguotou, Maotai and Wuliangye are much more expensive. Other than these white spirit, there are yellow spirit or Huangjiu which are lower in alcoholic content, the alcoholic content is usually around 16%.

Most visitors will want to try Peking duck and Mongolian hot pot. Founded in 1864, Quanjude Roast Duck Restaurant is one of the city's most popular Peking duck restaurants. There are six restaurants in the chain, but the most convenient one is the original one, just five minute walk south of Tiananmen Square. Address: 32 Qianmen Dajie, (010) 65112418.

The flavor of Mongolian hot pot is like fondue but without cheese. Besides meat and vegetables, there are fish balls, noodles, tofu and so on for you to choose from. You can place your chosen food into the broth and pull them out with chopsticks or a ladle, and also you can skewer them, hold them in the broth until they are done to your liking. Dong Laishun has been famous for its hot pot for more than a century. Address: 34 Haidian Dajie, (010) 62560556. Near the Tiananmen Square, the more inquisitive visitor will find Wangfujng Street market where he or she can experience foods from all over China, such as barbecues, cheese, spicy noodles and so on.

In the past, Beijing People liked to eat boiled thin slices of mutton in a seasoned broth. But recently,

Cantonese and Sichuan flavor hot pots have become more popular. Thinly sliced beef, mutton and fresh vegetables are the basic ingredients of a hotpot. In some hot pot restaurants (火锅店), you can add sea food such as shrimps, lobsters, etc.

The meat and vegetables are boiled in the broth, and after being cooked thoroughly, they are dipped into the condiments. The flavor of the Cantonese hot pot is relatively mild while the Sichuan hot pot is so spicy that your tongue may feel numb a little bit.

But now in many places the buffet style hot pot is very popular. In an "all you can eat" environment, you can choose any hot pot ingredients, condiments and broth seasonings you like.

A style of Chinese food which is called Imperial Court Food originated from the Imperial Palace. 150 years ago, you were definitely not able to try this food, which was only served to Emperors. Now the best ones are served in Fang Shan in Beihai Park and in Ting Li Guan in the Summer Palace. Why not give it a try?

Chinese people love to eat. There are numerous restaurants everyone and you will have a hard time to find a street that has no restaurant. You can of course eat in some restaurants in your hotel. They usually serve English food menu and western food. The price can be a little expensive. If you want to save money and still want to see what local Chinese people love to eat, then go out to eat. In some restaurants, you can choose food ingredients from water tanks, cages and shelves to specify what you want. If you can't communicate clearly with the waiter or waitress, just point at some meals you

think you may want to try on other people's table.

In this book, we will not list many individual restaurants because there are just too many to list. Instead, we list some very famous gourmet streets. In these gourmet streets, there are numerous restaurants with different food flavors. We bet you will find the food you like best. How to find a very good restaurant? Here is a tip. Follow the majority. If you find a very crowded and busy restaurant, most likely it is a very good restaurant. The local Chinese know which one restaurant is better.

The following are some of the famous gourmet streets in Beijing:

1) In north part of Beijing, not far from the Olympic Green area, there is a gourmet street, its address: Huizhong Lu,Yayuncun亚运村慧忠路.

2) Located in Fucheng Lu, it is called Chaoji Dafan gourmet street 阜成路"超级大饭"一条街

3) Located in Qicai Bei Lu, there is a new gourmet street called Laitai gourmet street 莱太美食街.

4) Located in Suzhou Jie 苏州街 in Zhongguancun area, you will find that there are many highly educated professionals eating here since Zhongguancun is an area where there are many high tech companies. You can probably find some Chinese people who can speak English well here.

5) Located in Qianmen Dajie 前门大街, in this gourmet street you can find Quanjude Roast Duck restaurant and other famous restaurants with over one hundred years of history. It is near the Tian'anmen square.

6) Located in Guanganmen 广安门, in this gourmet street, you will find many Sichuan style restaurant. If you like hot food, you may try this place.

Traditional Chinese Food

Shanghai and other Olympic cities

In other Olympic cities, you will find different types of foods. For instance, in Qingdao and Qinhuangdao, the seafood is very famous. Many restaurants specialize in seafood. The tastes are quite different from Chinatown in western countries. If you really want to enjoy your trip, just try some of the true Chinese food. Here we list some famous gourmet streets, where you can find many restaurants to fill your stomach. You will feel amazed at the number of different types of food they offer.

FOOD AND ENTERTAINMENT

Shanghai

There are several famous gourmet streets in Shanghai. Local Shanghai people go to eat in Yunnan Lu云南路美食街a lot. Here you can find food which originates from other areas such as Beijing, Guangzhou, etc. Other famous streets include Huanghe Lu黄河路 and Zapu Lu乍浦路 in Hongkou District.

Tianjin

In Tianjin, the famous gourmet street is in Binjiang Lu 滨江道, near Xinhua Road. Another one is in Nansi Shipin Jie南市食品街

Shenyang

In Shenyang, one of the famous gourmet streets is located in Zhong Jie 中街小吃一条街. Zhong Jie is also a famous commercial street in Shenyang.

Qingdao

The famous gourmet street in Qingdao is in Minjiang Lu闽江路美食街.

Qinhuangdao

In Qinhuangdao, one of the famous gourmet streets is in the fifth floor of Jinyuan Shopping Mall金原商厦五楼.

Western Restaurants in China

Beijing

Restaurants offering food of American, Brazilian, French, German, Indian, Japanese, Italian, etc. can be found everywhere in Beijing.

As a modern big city, Beijing offers a great variety of western and non-Chinese dishes. For instance, American, French, Indian, Italian and Brazilian food can be found everywhere in Beijing. Those dishes could meet the  increasing demand of the foreign visitors and make all the people both from home and abroad satisfied. In addition, there are a lot of fast food options, which make your shopping expedition much more convenient, all major established chain stores are available in Beijing. Many famous restaurants such as McDonald, Kentucky Fried Chicken, Pizza Hut, Starbuck's Coffee, Kentucky all have their chain stores here. Many restaurants are near the intersections or inside big shopping malls.

The following are western fast food restaurants that are very close to the Olympic Green area.

KFC 肯德基 - Beiyuan Road, Chaoyang District

McDonalds 麦当劳 - Anli Lu, Chaoyang District

Pizza Hut 必胜客 - Zhongguancun Jie, Haidian District

Starbuck's Coffee 星巴克 - 309 Huizhongbeili, Chaoyang District

Subway 赛百味 - 44 Kexueyuan Nan Lu, Haidian District

Shanghai

Near Shanghai stadium, there are many western restaurants, such as McDonald, Pizza Hut. In Caoxi Lu 漕溪路, you can find Papa John's, McDonalds, Pizza Hut, etc.

in 70 Zhongshan Lu中山路. In 72 XianggangZhong Lu, you can find one Starbuck's shop in a very famous shopping mall called Jiashike.

缤纷世界...

多彩生活...

Fun World
colorful life...

Qingdao

One Pizza Hut is located in 10 Xianggang Zhong Lu, it is near the famous travel attractions Qingdao 54 square and music square. One McDonalds is located

Shenyang

You can find McDonald restaurant in 83 Changjiang Jie, Huanggu District 长江街. One Pizza Hut restaurant can be found in 201 Zhongjie Lu, Shenhe District中街路, on the same street, you can find a Starbuck's coffee shop.

Qinhuangdao

In Haiyang Lu 海阳路, you can find a McDonald restaurant.

Tianjin

In Bing Jiang Dao, there is a pizza hut restaurant which is pretty new. It is close to the Le Bin Shopping Center. KFC is next to it.

Bars and Night Life

Beijing

There are a lot of bars and night clubs in Beijing. The most famous bars are in the Sanlitun bar Street 三里屯酒吧街. These bars often have live music and performance shows. In some bars, the language is English. So if you want to relax a little bit and talk with someone who can speak English, going to the bars is a good choice.

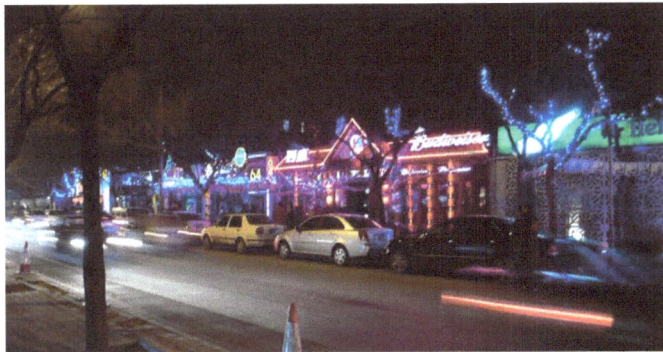

Shanghai

Bars offer a much relaxed environment after your busy travel in Shanghai. You can watch live music bands performing and drink your favorite wine.

The biggest bar street in Shanghai is in Hengshan Lu衡山路.Because it is near the foreign embassies in Shanghai, you might feel that you are in a foreign country. Other famous bar streets include Maoming Nan Lu茂名南路, Julu Lu巨鹿路 and the bund. There are many foreign people there.

Tianjin

The most famous bar street in Tianjin is in Youyi Lu友谊路.

Shenyang

Famous bar streets in Shenyang include Sanjing Jie三经街 and Fengtian Jie 奉天街.

Qingdao

The bar streets in Minjiang 2 Lu闽江二路 is famous.

Qinhuangdao

The most famous bars are in Haigang District. One example is Maisha Bar 麦沙酒吧 in Jin Jie.

7 SHOPPING

Buying Olympic Mascots

The Fuwa (福娃) are the official mascots of the 2008 Summer Olympic Games. They carry the messages of friendship and peace, along with good wishes from China to children all over the world. Fuwa use the five

colors of the Olympic rings in their design. The design combines the natural characteristics of the four most popular animals in China: the Panda, the Tibetan Antelope, the Fish and the Swallow, with the playfulness and camaraderie of five small children along with the Olympic Flame. Fuwa have a rhyming to syllable names in line with the traditional Chinese way of expressing affection for children. Beibei is the Fish, Huanhuan is the Olympic Flame, Yingying is the Tibetan Antelope, Jingjing is the Panda, and Nini is the Swallow. Combining their names, Fuwa, the young ambassadors for the Olympic Games, are saying 'Bei Jing Huan Ying Ni', which means 'Welcome to Beijing'. Fuwa also represent the landscape, and the dreams and aspirations of people from every corner of China.

Fuwa take the traditional Chinese good wishes wherever they go. Since ancient times in China, expression of good wishes has often taken the form of signs or symbols, such as figurines of mythical characters associated with positive attributes. Wherever they go, Beibei, Jingjing, Huanhuan,

Yangyang, and Nini carry hopes for a world of prosperity, happiness, passion, health and good luck.

Above all, Fuwa are designed to reflect the Olympic spirit, and unite the world in peace and friendship. The Beijing 2008 Olympics has a theme of "One world, One Dream", and Fuwa show the deep desire of the Chinese people to extend a friendly hand to every nation. They offer an invitation to everyone, everywhere to embrace this spirit together, with the light of the Olympic torch leading the way.

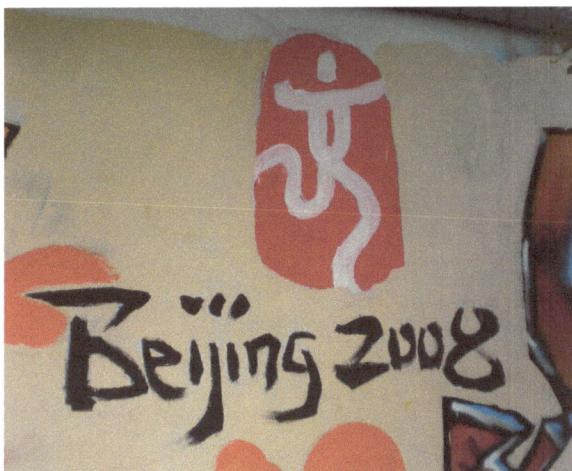

Official 2008 Olympics merchandise is sold at special stores throughout China, which started to appear in 2007. By the beginning of August in 2007 over 800 of these stores had been opened. Since then, Olympic memorabilia has been made available online at http://www.2008eshop.cn within China, or http://www.bj2008eshop.com for international purchases. Thousands of products are available, from Fuwa dolls to Olympic flags. You can also buy Beijing Olympic products online from Amazon (http://www.amazon.com), using keywords such as "Beijing 2008 Olympics" for your search.

Shopping in Beijing

In Beijing there are seemingly countless shopping complexes. Xidan, Oriental Plaza, Haidian, Qianmen Dashilan, Wangfujin, Guomao, and Zhongguancun Square are among the names of popular shopping areas, each usually having a degree of specialization. Good food will always be within steps, and the prices are very low to Western budgets.

It is not hard to find street vendors with a few real or manufactured antiques in

Beijing, but those who really love to collect antiques will want to visit Liulichang and/or Panjiayuan Antique City, where musty must-haves are found at every turn. Likewise, one can find bargains on fine clothing throughout the city but for top quality export fashions at prices well below what you pay in New York or Paris, be sure to reserve some time to explore the Yaxiu clothing market and Xiushui Street. Pearl, jade, and handmade jewelry, fine silk, electronics, kites, knives, small pottery items, and many other knick-knacks can be gifts over a range of prices, but always sure to be inexpensive compared to 'back home'. Of course, the buyer must be careful, as there are unscrupulous vendors, but even among the good ones, it is expected that the initial quoted price is a bit wishful.

In Beijing, shopping can take a lot of your time. Like most big cities, you can find nearly everything in Beijing. Be ready to be insistent though, as bargaining is expected in many shopping situations, and tourists are readily identifiable and sometimes viewed as the potential source of a windfall profit.

As mentioned, each Beijing market often has a more-or-less dominant specialty, such as electronics, antiques, or clothing. Panjiayuan Market (also known as the 'Weekend Market') is Beijing's largest market, with particularly large numbers of hand-crafted, antique and decorative items. The Liulicang market, on the other hand, has enormous numbers of old and new books for sale, as well as paintings and custom stamps while you wait. Computers, audio devices, and similar gadgets can are found concentrated in the Zhongguancun market, but be ready to be hawked!

The procedure in some shopping centers is: after you decided what you want to purchase, the assistant will write an invoice which you present to the cashier and make your payment; you then take the stamped receipt to the assistant to collect the item you have purchased.

Fixed-price selling is sometimes seen, but haggling is the norm in any street market transaction, as well as most other stores. It is not unusual for a seller to more than double his expected price in the initial offering, especially if there is a perception that you are ignorant of price norms. Try to take it in stride, and even enjoy the process. However if it is not for you, then more pricey, but less stressful shopping can be found at fixed-price stores, such as Malls at Oriental Plaza.

OPEN

营业中

We Proudly Accept

DISCOVER
NETWORK

UnionPay
银联

Famous Business Streets

You should not be surprised to see special events at larger shopping centers, such as concerts, acrobats, or fashion shows. From the Silk Market (Xiushui) to Xidan, there is something for everyone, and then SOGO, Lufthansa, Chung-yo, and Wangfujing are others among the favorite shopping areas. The open-air markets are quite exciting, with all manner of sounds, smells and sights. Of course, such markets often include merciless marketing, so be prepared to stand firm, buying what you want and nothing more, at a fair price.

Here we introduce some famous business streets where you can buy many products you like.

Shopping in Beijing

Xidan

Shopping, dining and an entertainment environment can be found at Chung-Yo Department Store and the Xidan Market. Business at Chung-Yo's is more often than not rather rapid. There are promotions in each month. Xidan is a shopper's paradise, discounted prices ease open even the tightest wallets. Great music, fashions and plenty of the world's famous brand products are evidence of Beijing's ever-increasing cosmopolitan presence.

Wangfujing

Built during the Ming dynasty, this street has a history of setting trends. Now it has been transformed into a shopping mall. The mall is pedestrian only with the exception of bus services. Beijing Department Store is the best-known store in this area. One World Department Store, which is to the north of it, stocks quality products and collections of Chinese and foreign famous brands. The largest market in Beijing, covering 100,000 square meters, is Sundong'an Market. Over 200,000 kinds of goods may be purchased there.

THE MALLS AT
ORIENTAL PLAZA

东方新天地

The Silk Market

Don't be misled by the name, there is more than just silk on sale at "The Silk Market". Silk products are inexpensive and popular, but shoes, leather goods, cashmere garments, watches, and some handicrafts are also sold here. Dozens of stores line the Xiushui Street. The products are often over priced, foreigners are recommended to be accompanied by a Chinese friend who can help negotiate the best possible price. It is located near the Friendship Shop and the embassy area and is very popular with foreign visitors. Perusing the narrow lanes in a laid-back manner and viewing the beautiful garments will quickly stimulate your passion for shopping. If you're looking for treasures here, then bargaining is a must and is expected.

Qianmen

One of the favorite shopping area local people like to go is the Dashilan Street in Qianmen area. It was a commercial center over 500 years ago and now is treasured for its small stalls.

Silver Street

If you are looking for franchised foreign name-brand shops, then look no further than Silver Street, located in the Dongdan Beidajie.

Hongqiao Market

Northern China's largest pearl distribution center is, Hongqiao Market, and it is well-known nationally and internationally. More than 1000 stores are located in this 32,000 square meter building which has three floors below ground level and five floors above ground level. The market is advanced with highly functional, practical facilities, high storage space capabilities. The Hongqiao Market area also has hotels, restaurants, office buildings, banking and postal services. Hongqiao Market enjoys a good reputation for the quality of its merchandise, its fair prices and considerate service. Foreigners are very much welcome. The jewelry fair at Beijing Hongqiao International Jewel Center is never ending.

Jianguomenwai Dajie

Lined up with restaurants, shopping centers, office buildings and beauty salons, Jianguomenwai Dajie is known for its colorful urban scene. Guiyou Department Store, Friendship Store, SCITECH Plaza and the China World Shopping Mall, are all renowned shopping centers.

Shopping Center Directory in Beijing

Beijing Department Store
Address: 255 Wangfujing Dajie

Landao Shopping Center
Address: 8 Chaoyangmenwai Dajie

China World Shopping Mall
Address: 1 Jianwai Dajie

Chang'an Department Store
Address: 15 Fuxinmenwai Dajie

Beijing Guiyou Shopping Mall
Address: A5 Jianguomenwai Dajie

Chung-Yo Department Store
Address: 178 Xidan Beijie

Shopping in Shanghai

Shanghai is China's largest commercial city. There are shops everywhere within walking distance. Here we introduce some famous shopping areas in Shanghai.

Famous Business Streets

Nanjing Road

Nanjing Road is a very famous shopping street in China. It lines up with more than 600 shops. It is the largest shopping center in Shanghai.

Huaihai Road

Huaihai Road is another well known

business street for shopping. There are at least 400 stores over there.

Huating Road

It is a street full of clothes and decoration stores. The fashion trend in Shanghai starts from right here.

Dongtai Road

Here you can find classic handicrafts such as ceramics, jade, paintings, calligraphic works, etc. This market is world famous.

Yuyuan Tourist Trade City

Next to the famous Yuyuan Garden is the famous Yuyuan Tourist Trade City. Here many shops sell small commodities. Here you can go shopping, enjoy delicious food, see beautiful scenery and have fun.

Shopping Center Directory in Shanghai

Pacific Department Store
Address: 932 Hengshan Lu

Huaqiao Department Store
Address: 627 Nanjing Dong Lu

The Hongkou Commercial Mansions
Address: 838 Sichuan Bei Lu

Duolun Commercial Mansions
Address: 1885 Sichuan Bei Lu
Guanghui Square
Address: 1 Hongqian Lu

Liankafo Commerical Mansions

Address: 93 Huaihai Lu
Shanghai Silk Market
Address: 139 Tianping Lu

Shopping in Qingdao

If you drink beer, you probably have heard Tsingtao Beer. This world famous beer is from Qingdao. In this beautiful coastal city, you can find

many things suitable for souvenirs such as shell carvings, Laoshan Tea, diamond ornaments and straw crafts. Here the famous business street is located in Zhongshan Lu; it is next to the famous Qingdao Pier. You won't miss it.

Shopping Center Directory in Qingdao

Qingdao Zhongshan Commercial Street

Address: Zhongshan Lu

Dongtai Jusco Shopping Center

Address: 72 Hong Kong Zhong Lu

Hisense (Haixin) Plaza

Address: 9 Shangdong Lu

Qingdao Department Store

Address: 51 Zhongshan Lu

Qingdao Culture Market

Address: Changle Lu

Hong Ren Tang Pharmacy

Address: 196 Zhongshan Lu

Fada Department Store

Address: 12 Zhongshan Lu

Shopping in Qingdao

Shopping in Qinhuangdao

Shopping Center Directory in Qinhuangdao

Qinxin Shopping Center (秦新百货)

Address: 138 Hebei Dajie

Hualian Shopping Center (华联)

Address: 17 Wenhua Bei Lu

Qinhuangdao Commercial City (秦皇岛商城)

Address: 152 Hebei Dajie

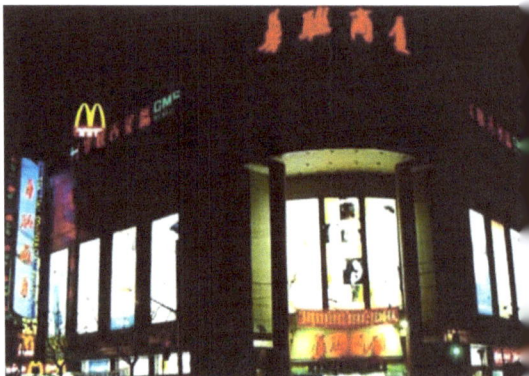

Shopping in Shenyang

Shopping Center Directory in Shenyang

Wal-Mart Super Center (沃尔玛)

Address: No.9, Zhonghua Lu, Heping District

Pakson Shopping Center (百盛购物中心)

Address: 21 Zhonghua Lu

Baijia Shopping Center (百佳购物中心)

Address: Heping District

Bailian Shopping Center (百联购物中心)

Address: 55 Qingnian Dajie

Shopping in Tianjin

Shopping Center Directory in Tianjin

Binhai Shopping Center (滨海商场)

Address: Jiefang Lu

Wuhuan Shopping Center (五环商场)

Address: Yangliuqing, Xiqing District

Baisheng Shopping Center (百盛购物中心)

Address:162 Heping Lu

Yinzou Shopping Center (银座购物中心)

Address: 143 Binjiang Dao

How to Negotiate the Price

In China bargaining is commonplace. What appears to be a loud heated argument, involving distressed facial expressions are in fact just intense negotiations. It's a big game, the purchaser must be ready to walk away if the quoted price is higher than the 'fair price' they had in mind.

If you don't like to haggle, you may go directly to the department stores or supermarkets. The prices there are normally fixed, no room for negotiation. If you want to get a good deal and buy the stuff you want a little bit cheaper, then you need to negotiate with many

shop owners. Otherwise you may get ripped off. Many street vendors, small shops owners expect you to negotiate with them and already set the price higher so that they can still make profits after negotiation. So negotiation is a must. Actually negotiation is a very important business skill in the world. If you own a house, you probably dealt with the contractors who repair your floor or roof. Did you negotiate with them? We bet you did. If you had been to some yard sale, you may also have some negotiation experience. Now you have the opportunity to practice your negotiation skills in China! From the bargaining experience, you will learn that China is now really in market economy, many Chinese businessmen are good at negotiation.

For some of you who may feel a little headache when negotiating with the sellers, here we provide some tips to help you out.

Don't reveal how much you would like to pay for an article unless the sale is reaching its conclusion. Before naming a price, endeavor to lower seller's offering price as much as possible. Do shout out unrealistic low prices, like 10 RMB just as long as you can keep a big smile on your face. Do keep that smile going throughout the transaction. The vendor is a great deal more likely to keep on bargaining when he sees a happy smiling face. Conversely, getting angry seldom gets you the price you desire.

Do research the value of the item you're after; ask Chinese friends, hotel staff, foreign residents for some advice. If you really want to buy something, a useful approach is to pretend to walk off. You can say, "Sorry, I am not interested", or "I need to go now".

If you get called back, you know you are close to a deal. If the call doesn't come, go to a comparable shop, and try again but with a slightly higher bid.

English words which you hear being spoken by the vendors will often consist of "how much you pay", "good quality" and the vendors often use a jumbo calculator to show you the price to make sure you understand them clearly. The best method is to keep repeating 'cheaper' as often as possible, before revealing the price you have in mind. Give the vendor a price of approximately 40% of the price you fixed on, and go up in 5% increments until he or she capitulates.

8 PRACTICAL TRAVEL TIPS

温馨提示
WARNINGS

让优美的环境追随我们的脚步
Please protect the environment

讲文明游区团聚
Please behave in a good manner

保护文物古迹就是我们大家共同的责任
Please protect the cultural relics

走进什刹海·感受老北京
Feel Old Beijing in Shichahai

同一个世界 同一个梦想
One World One Dream

Climate

The following is the average temperature (Highest/Lowest) in Fahrenheit for all of the Olympic cities in mainland China. Prepare your clothes accordingly before your travel.

Month	Beijing	Shanghai	Tianjin	Qingdao	Qinhuangdao	Shenyang
Jan	34/15	45/32	34/18	36/22	32/6	22/2
Feb	39/19	47/34	39/22	38/27	38/12	28/8
Mar	52/30	54/41	52/33	47/35	50/26	43/24
Apr	67/45	65/51	67/47	57/45	66/42	60/38
May	79/55	74/60	79/58	67/55	79/53	73/52
Jun	86/64	81/68	86/67	73/63	84/62	80/61
Jul	87/70	88/76	87/72	80/71	86/69	84/68
Aug	85/68	88/76	86/71	82/73	85/66	82/66
Sep	78/57	81/68	78/61	76/65	77/53	74/53
Oct	66/45	72/58	67/49	67/55	66/40	60/39
Nov	50/31	62/47	51/34	54/42	40/26	42/24
Dec	37/19	51/36	38/22	41/30	36/12	28/9

Time Difference

China uses Beijing time across the whole country. Beijing time is eight hours ahead of Greenwich Mean Time (GMT). If you are still confused, you can check the website http://www.timeanddate.com to find the exact date and time.

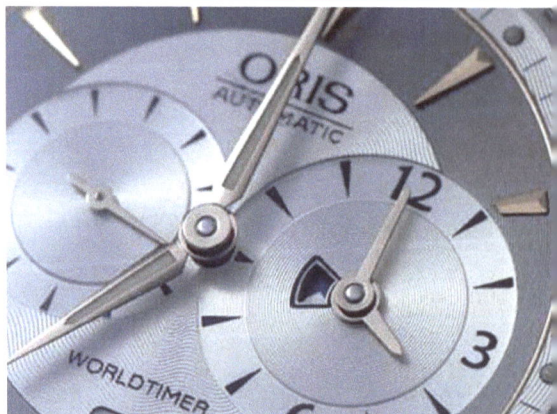

Unit Conversion

Chinese people use the international metric system. So you need to know how to convert the numbers from metric system to your familiar system. Here are some useful formulas for your reference.

1 meter = 3 feet 3 inches, 1 centimeter = 0.4 inches, 1 kilometer=0.6 miles

100 grams= 3.53 ounces, 1 kilogram =2.2 pounds, 1 liter=0.76 pint, 1 US gallon=3.8 L

In some shopping areas, Chinese people use old weights system of Jin (斤) and Liang (两).

1 Jin=0.6 kg=1.32 lbs, 1 Liang=37.5 g=1.32 oz.

If You Are Lost

Just ask a local Chinese. As we said, young students know some English. If you cannot find young students, you may show any local Chinese a map and point to where you want to go. They will point you to the right direction. If you still get stuck, then take a taxi to go to your hotel. In your hotel, ask the front desk how to go to the destination and ask them to write the destination in Chinese characters so that you may show to other people if you are lost again. Another way is to find a subway station and take the subway to the closest station near your destination. Then take a taxi, this will save you some money. Be alert when you want to cross any intersection, watch out for cars or bicycles.

Rest Room

In big cities such as Beijing and Shanghai, there are many clean public rest rooms. The government has spent a lot of money in recent years to improve the quality of the public rest rooms. Many star level hotels have western style rest rooms. If you use the public rest rooms, make sure that you bring some toilet paper with you. Look for "WC" signs near the intersections to find the directions to go to the rest rooms.

Carry Important Documents

You need to keep a copy of your important documents at home and carry one with you. **You are required to carry your passport at all times because the police regularly carry out random checks.** Usually you can find a business center in your hotel where you can use copy machines to make copies of your documents. If you forgot to do so in your hotel, you can find a copy center to copy them. For instance, you can use Kinko's. Kinko's is the American's famous photocopy center where people can make copies, send fax, etc. In Beijing, Kinko's also has its branch office. It is located in A11 Xiangjun Bei Lu, Beijing. Tel: (010) 65958020, Fax: (010) 65958218.

Tipping

Many travel guidebooks said no tipping is necessary. Actually, since more and more Chinese people travel abroad and know the common tipping practices in western countries, in many places in China, tipping is more than welcome and is rarely refused.

Medical Care

If you have medical emergency, you can contact SOS International. They offer 24-hour service. They can give you medical advice and refer you to some hospitals. In Beijing, its phone number is: (010) 64629100. In Shanghai, its phone number is: (021) 62950099. You can also ask your hotel front desk for help in such situations.

In case you get sick during your travel, we provide some information about the hospitals, pharmacies and dental clinics in the Olympic host cites including Beijing, Shanghai, Tianjin, Shenyang, Qingdao and Qinhuangdao.

Beijing

Beijing United Family Hospital

Address: 2 Jiang Tai Lu, Chaoyang District

Tel: (010) 64333960 or 64333961

Golden Elephant Pharmacy

Address: 277 Wangfujing Dajie

Tel: (010) 65229135

Haisheng Dental Clinic

Address: Building 10, Anhua Xi Lu, first floor

Tel: (010) 64254777

Shanghai

Shanghai First People's Hospital International Medical Care Center

Address: 585 Jiu Long Lu

Tel: (021) 63240090 ext 2101

Dental Clinic

Address: 666 Changle Lu

Tel: (021) 62477386

Qingdao

International Clinic of Qingdao Municipal Hospital

Address: 5 DongHai Zhong Lu

Tel: (0532) 85937690 ext. 2266

web: http://www.qd-hospital.com.cn

Huaqing International Medical Healthcare Centre

Addr: 97 Xianggang Dong Lu, Qingdao, China

Tel: (0532) 88017770

Email: hq_imhc@sina.com

Medical Care

Medical Care and Health Centre for Women and Children

Addr: 27 Wuding Lu

Tel: (0532) 82857555

David Dental Clinic (54 Square Office)

Address: F3-1A Binhai Garden, 33 DongHai Xi Lu

Tel: (0532) 85721822

web: http://www.daviddental.cn

Email: info@daviddental.cn

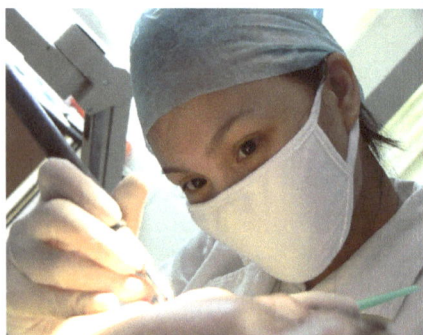

Qinhuangdao

Haigang Hospital

Address: 131 Wenhua Bei Lu

Tel: (0335)3031063

Baoshantang Pharmacy

Address: 137 Hebei Dajie Dong Duan

Tel: (0335) 3142180

Tianjin

Tianjin No.1 Center Hospital

Address: 24 Fukang Lu

Tel: (022)23626600

Hongcheng Pharmacy

Address: 47 Qiongzhou Dao, Hexi District

Tel: (022) 23233991

Shenyang

The People's Hospital of Liaoning Province

Address: 33 Wenyi Lu, Shenhe District

Tel: (024)24147900

AMBULANCE: (024) 24810136/24147900

Tagami Dental Clinic

Address: Gate 4, 99 Nan Ta Jie, Dongling District

Tel: (024)24561295; 24561289

Emergency call No.: 13998322258

American Medical Center-Global Doctor Medical Staff

Address: 54 Pangjiang Lu, Dadong District

Tel: (024)24330678, 24326409

Fax: (024)24331008

Emergency call: (024)24326409

Useful Phone Numbers and Websites

Fire 119

Police 110

Medical emergencies 120

Traffic accidents and reports 122

Red Cross emergency aid line 999

Directory Assistance 114

Weather forecast 12121

Beijing Hygiene Supervision Department Hotline 12320

Beijing Judicial Bureau 148 for Legal Services 12348

Beijing Municipal General Administration and Law-Enforcement Bureau Hotline 96310

Beijing Municipality Entry/Exit question hotline 26611266

Beijing Municipality Entry/Exit information hotline 84020101

Beijing Municipal Government's Public Hotline 12345

Beijing Industry and Commerce Administration Line for Filing Complaints 12315

Beijing Quality and Technical Supervision Bureau Complaint Line 12365

Beijing Consumer Association complaint line 62241234

Beijing Municipal Tourist hotline 65130828

Beijing Quality and Technology Control Bureau Website: http://www.bjtsb.gov.cn

Beijing Entry/Exit Inspection &

Quarantine Website: http://www.bjciq.gov.cn

Beijing Hygiene Information Website: http://www.bjhb.gov.cn

Beijing Government Foreign Affairs Office Website: http://www.bjfao.gov.cn

Official Olympic Ticketing Service Website: http://tickets.beijing2008.com

Beijing Public Security Bureau Website: http://www.bjgaj.gov.cn

Beijing General Administration and Law Enforcement Bureau Website: http://www.bjcg.gov.cn

In addition, it is helpful to know how to contact your embassies in China.

Safety

China is a safe place to travel. You normally should not worry too much about your personal safety. Chinese people are friendly. Sometimes, some Chinese people may stare at you, they are just curious about foreigners, nothing else. Do not get offended about it. In some busy travel attractions or crowded area, watch out for your belongings. Avoid walking alone in quiet streets after dark. It is better to find a partner to go with you in such situations. Crimes seldom happen to foreign visitors. If caught, the criminals can face very severe penalties.

Water and Air Quality

In general, use bottled water. The tap water is usually not suitable to drink. The bottled water is cheap to buy nearly anywhere on the streets. Some hotels offer boiled water in a flask or thermos daily in your room, it is ok to drink the boiled water.

China has taken measures to improve the air quality. In Beijing, the air quality has improved a lot. In coastal cities such as Qingdao, you may feel even better air quality. This issue had been exaggerated in the past; in fact the air quality should not be your concern.

Keep Friendly

In China, dignity is very important. People like those who respect them. If you are in a situation that you want to argue with the Chinese people, it is better to keep friendly and do not confront the other person aggressively. Just try to ask the other party to help you solve the problem you have. Don't fight or shout, Chinese people like polite and friendly guests.

Hope you enjoy your Olympic tour of China!

PRACTICAL TRAVEL TIPS

APPENDIX

How to pronounce the Chinese Pinyin

A crash course

Pinyin, literally it means 'spell out the sound'. It's a system for romanizing Chinese characters used in mainland China for Mandarin, it is also called putonghua. Chinese pinyin has four tones. If you are new to Chinese, just do not worry about the tones for now. If you want to learn more about tones, you can learn them later. For now, you can ignore the tones. Just remember to practice the pronunciation for the following letters in pinyin, you will be fine.

A as a in "far"

E as a in "amount"

I as e in "eat"

O as o in "rock"

U as oo in "too"

C as ts in "cats"

Q as ch in "chess"

X as sh in "She"

Z as ds in "seeds"

ZH as j in "Joe"

CH as ch in "chop"

R as s in "pleasure"

AI as I in "hi"

AO as ou in "ouch"

EI as ay in "hay"

IU sounds like "you"

OU as oe in "toe"

UI as ay in "way"

English-Chinese Phrase List

General

English	Pinyin	Chinese
What is your name?	Ni jiao shen ma?	你叫什么名字?
Hello	Ni hao	你好
Goodbye	Zai jian	再见
Thank you	Xie xie	谢谢
Sorry	Dui bu qi	对不起
Yes	Shi	是
No	Bu Shi	不是
Is it OK?	Ke yi ma?	可以吗

APPENDIX

Do you speak English?	Ni hui shuo ying yu ma?	你说英语吗
Do you understand it?	Ni dong ma?	你懂吗
I know.	Wo dong	我懂
I don't know.	Wo bu dong	我不懂
Where is the restroom?	Na you ce suo?	哪有厕所？
Please speak slowly.	Qing man dian shuo	请慢点说

Number

English	Pinyin	Chinese
1	Yi	一
2	Er	二
3	San	三
4	Si	四
5	Wu	五
6	Liu	六
7	Qi	七
8	Ba	八
9	Jiu	九
10	Shi	十
11	shi yi	十一
12	shi er	十二
13	shi san	十三
20	er shi	二十
21	er shi yi	二十一
22	er shi er	二十二
30	san shi	三十
40	si shi	四十
50	wu shi	五十
60	liu shi	六十
70	qi shi	七十
80	ba shi	八十
90	jiu shi	九十

| 100 | yi bai | 一百 |
| 1000 | yi qian | 一千 |

Directions

English	Pinyin	Chinese
East	Dong	东
West	Xi	西
South	Nan	南
North	Bei	北
Avenue	Dadao	大道
Street	Jie	街
Main Street	Dajie	大街
Road	Lu	路

Olympic Host City Names

English/Pinyin	Chinese	English/Pinyin	Chinese
Beijing	北京	Shanghai	上海
Tianjin	天津	Qingdao	青岛
Qinhuangdao	秦皇岛	Shenyang	沈阳

Time

English	Pinyin	Chinese
What time is it now?	Xian zai ji dian?	现在几点？
When	Shen mo shi hou	什么时候
Today	Jin tian	今天
Tomorrow	Ming tian	明天
Yesterday	Zuo tian	昨天
This morning	Jin tian zao shang	今天早上
This afternoon	Jin tian xia wu	今天下午
Tonight	Jin wan	今晚

Money

| English | Pinyin | Chinese |

I want to change my money to Chinese Yuan.	Wo yao huan RMB	我要兑换人民币
I want to cash the travelers check.	Wo yao dui huan zi piao	我要兑换旅行支票
Where I can find the nearest ATM machine?	Na you zi dong ti kuan ji?	哪有自动提款机
Where is the closest branch of Bank of China?	Zui jin de zhong guo yin hang zai na?	最近的中国银行在哪？

Telecommunication

English	Pinyin	Chinese
Where is the nearest post office?	Na you you dian ju?	哪有邮电局？
I want to buy a cell phone.	Wo yao mai shou ji	我要买手机
I want to buy a SIM card.	Wo yao mai SIM ka	我要买 SIM卡
Where is the nearest Internet café?	Na you wang ba?	哪有网吧？
Can anyone here speak English?	You ren jiang ying yu ma?	这里有人会讲英语吗？
Where can I use a telephone?	Na you dian hua?	哪有电话可用
May I use your phone? Thanks.	Ke yi yong ni de shou ji ma?	我可以用一下你的手机吗？
I want to buy some stamps	Wo yao mai you piao	我要买邮票

Hotel

English	Pinyin	Chinese
Do you still have hotel room available?	Hai you fang jian ma?	还有房间吗？
I want to stay for 2 days.	Wo yao zhu 2 tian	我要住2天
I want to find a travel agency.	Wo yao zhao lu xing she	我要找旅行社

Can you help to call a taxi for me?	Bang wo jiao liang chu zu che hao ma?	请帮我叫辆出租车
The air conditioner is too cold.	Kong tiao tai leng le	空调太冷
The air conditioner is too hot.	Kong tiao tai re	空调太热
How much does it cost per day?	Yi tian duo shao qian?	住一天多少钱？
Do you have standard room?	You biao zhun jian ma?	有标准间吗？
Single/Twin room	Dan ren chuang/shuang ren chuang	单人/ 双人房

Transportation

English	Pinyin	Chinese
Please use the taxi meter.	Qing da biao	请打里程表计费
How do I go to this address?	Wo zen mo dao zhe?	我怎么到这儿？
Is it far from here to there?	Li zhe yuan ma?	从这到那远吗？
How many minutes will it take?	Yao duo shao fen zhong?	需要多少分钟？
I want to go to the airport.	Wo yao qu ji chang	我要去机场
I want to go to my hotel. Here is the address.	Wo yao qu bin guan, zhe shi di zhi.	我要去宾馆，这是地址
I want to go to …	Wo yao qu …	我要去
I want to buy a ticket.	Wo yao mai piao	我要买票
Can I take this bus?	Wo ke yi zuo zhe liang che ma?	我可以坐这辆车吗？
Can I take this metro?	Wok e yi zuo zhe liang di tie ma?	我可以坐这趟地铁吗？
I didn't find my luggage, please help.	Wo de bao diu le, qing bang wo.	我的包丢了请帮忙

When is the next available flight?	Xia yi ban fei ji she mo shi hou?	下一班飞机什麽时候飞？
Turn left	Zuo zhuan	左转
Turn right	You zhuan	右转
Go straight	Zhi zhe zou	直着走
I am lost.	Wo mi lu le	我迷路了
Which station to get off?	Na zhan xi ache?	哪一站下车？
Where is the ticket office?	Na mai piao?	哪可以买票？
From … to …	Cong … dao …	从。。。到。。。
Entrance	Ru kou	入口
Exit	Chu Kou	出口
Stop here	Ting Che	停车
I want to get off here	Wo yao xia che	我要下车
Ticket office	Shou piao chu	售票处
Railway station	Huo che zhan	火车站
Bus station	Qi che zhan	汽车站
One-way ticket	Dan cheng piao	单程票
Return ticket	Wang fan piao	往返票
Timetable	Shi ke biao	时刻表

Shopping

English	Pinyin	Chinese
How much is this?	Duo shao qian?	多少钱
It is too expensive!	Tai gui la	太贵了
Cheaper Please!	Pian yi dian	请便宜点
I do not want it.	Wo bu yao	我不要
What is it?	Zhe shi shen mo?	这是什么？
Where can I get a …?	Na you …?	哪有。。。
Where can I buy a …?	Na ke yi mai …?	哪可以买。。。？
Can I look at that one?	Ke yi kan kan na ge ma?	可以看看那个吗？
Too big	Tai da	太大

To small	Tai xiao	太小
I need my change back because I overpaid you.	Qing zhao ling qian gei wo	请找零钱给我
Department store	Bai huo shang dian	百货商店
Shopping mall	Gou wu zhong xin	购物中心
Bookstore	Shu dian	书店
I want to get a map.	Wo yao yi zhang di tu	我要一张地图

Emergency

English	Pinyin	Chinese
Please call the police for me.	Qing bang wo jiao jing cha	请帮我叫警察
Can you help me?	Qing bang wo	请帮忙
Please help me.	Qing bang wo	请帮我
I have a diarrhea.	Wo la du zi	我拉肚子
I have fever.	Wo fa shao	我发烧了
I have headache.	Wo tou teng	我头疼
I do not feel comfortable.	Wo bu shu fu	我不舒服
Call a doctor for me please!	Qing jiao yi sheng	请帮我叫医生
I need to go to a hospital, please help!	Wo yao qu yi yuan	我要去医院，请帮忙
Please call an ambulance!	Qing jiao jiu hu che	请叫救护车
Where can I buy some medication?	Na ke yi mai yao?	哪可以买药

Food

English	Pinyin	Chinese
Restaurant	Can guan	餐馆
Upscale Restaurant	Fan dian/Jiu dian	饭店/酒店
Breakfast	Zao can	早餐
Lunch	Wu can	午餐

Dinner	Wan can	晚餐
Cheers!	Gan bei	干杯
Can I see your restaurant menu?	Wo yao kan cai dan	我要看菜单
I am a vegetarian.	Wo chi su	我吃素食
What food can I choose from?	You shen mo shi pin?	有什么食品？
What sweet cakes do you have?	You shen mo tian dian?	有什么甜食？
I need a fork, a knife and a spoon.	Wo yao cha zi, dao zi, shao zi	我要叉子，刀子，勺子
Do you have beer?	You pi jiu ma?	有啤酒吗？
Do you have wine?	You bai jiu ma?	有白酒吗？
Do you have orange juice?	You ju zi zhi ma?	有橘子汁吗？
Do you have lemonade juice?	You ning meng zhi ma?	有柠檬汁吗？
I need a bottle of water.	Wo yao yi ping shui	我要一瓶水
Do you have hot (spicy) food?	You la de cai ma?	有辣的菜吗？
Is this food hot?	Zhe cai la ma?	这菜辣吗？
Do you have western food?	You xi can ma?	有西餐吗？
Do you have any fruit?	You shui guo ma?	有水果吗？
Please don't use Soy sauce.	Qing bu yao yong jiang you	请别用酱油
I need a cup of coffee.	Wo yao ka fei	我要咖啡
I need rice.	Wo yao mi fan	我要米饭
Do you have salt?	You yan ma?	有盐吗？
Do you have seafood?	You hai huo ma?	有海货吗？
Do you have ice cream?	You bing ji ling ma?	有冰激凌吗？
Please do not add MSG in the food.	Qing bie jia wei jing	请别加味精
I want to check out.	Wo yao jie zhang	我要结帐

Index

APPENDIX

Index

APPENDIX

Index

APPENDIX

X

Y